Triumphs of the Heart

Triumphs of the Heart

Miraculous True Stories of the Power of Love

CHRIS BENGUHE

A Perigee Book

A Perigee Book
Published by The Berkley Publishing Group
A division of Penguin Putnam Inc.
375 Hudson Street
New York, New York 10014

First edition: August 2000

Published simultaneously in Canada.

The Penguin Putnam Inc. World Wide Web site address is
http://www.penguinputnam.com

Library of Congress Cataloging-in-Publication Data

Benguhe, Chris.
Triumphs of the heart : miraculous true stories of the power of love /
Chris Benguhe.
1st ed.
p.cm
ISBN 0-399-52613-7
1. Love—Case Studies. I. Title.

BF575.L8 B37 2000
152.4'1—dc21   00-029670

Printed in the United States of America

10   9   8   7   6   5   4   3   2

To Babycat with Love

Contents

Acknowledgments

~

As a young man growing up in Arizona and dreaming of one day changing the world for the better, in one way or another, I was overwhelmed with confusion over just how I was ever going to get anyone to listen to anything I had to say.

But there were special people in my life who knew how much I wanted to make a difference and helped me in whatever way they could. They all played a crucial part in enabling me to become a writer and tell these inspiring stories of love, as well as teaching me that the most important things in life are people and the support and love we give each other.

To that end I wish to thank Phyllis Benguhe, John

and Glenda Benguhe, my brothers John Benguhe and Philip Benguhe; my mentors Father John Becker S.J., Stephen Geller, Tony Frost, Bob Smith, and my supportive friend Juliet Barkanyi. And most important, I thank the inspiring love of my life, Carol Storms.

Last, but certainly not least, thanks to my agents becker & mayer!, my supportive and helpful editor, Jennifer Repo, my research assistant, Kathryn Pease, and to all the willing subjects whose courage and love in the face of tremendous adversity inspired me to write this book and will hopefully encourage millions around the world.

Introduction
George W. Bush

꠵

Throughout my campaign I've carried the message that our country must be prosperous. And a prosperous America should have a purpose—to make sure the American dream touches every heart and leaves no one behind. But in order to make this a reality, we must be not only a wealthy nation, but also one that is rich in compassion and love.

The reality is that often when a life is broken, it can only be rebuilt by another caring, concerned human being. Someone whose actions say, "I love you, I believe in you. I'm in your corner." This is compassion with a human face and a human voice. It is not an isolated act—it is a personal relationship. And it works. There simply is no substitute for unconditional love and personal contact.

I was saddened recently by the story of a gang initiation in Michigan. A fifteen-year-old boy endured two minutes of vicious beatings from other members without fighting back. He was then required to stand up and embrace his attackers. When asked why he allowed himself to be tortured this way, he answered, "I knew this was going to hurt really bad, but I felt that if I could take it for just a couple of minutes, I'd be surrounded by people who loved me."

Imagine a young life that desperate for real love. And multiply it by millions. This crisis of the spirit creates an expanding circle of responsibility. We are responsible for loving our neighbors as we want to be loved ourselves.

Parents must understand that being good moms or dads should be their highest goal in life. Congregations and community groups must fight for children and neighborhoods, creating what Pope John Paul II calls, "a hospitable society, a welcoming culture."

A president has responsibilities, too. A president can speak for accountability and the power of faith and love. Though government can spend money, it can't put hope in our hearts or give meaning to our lives. This is done by the churches, synagogues, mosques and charities that fill this sometimes cold world with warmth. But most important, it is through people helping each other to create a quiet river of goodness and kindness that can cut through stone.

This is exactly what the devoted mothers and fathers, brothers, sisters and friends in these triumphant stories accomplished with their love and loyalty—they have cut through stones of hardship and adversity to bring about miracles of compassion.

As Americans, this is our mission. We stumble and splinter when we forget that. We unite and prosper when we remember it. No great calling is ever easy, and no work of man is ever perfect. But we can, in our imperfect way, rise now and again to the example of Saint Francis—where there is hatred, sowing love; where there is darkness, shedding light; where there is despair, bringing hope.

Governor George W. Bush, 2000, by permission of the George W. Bush for President Campaign.

Love's Long Burn

*I*t was a typical hot and sweltering Chicago day in August 1972 when the emergency call came over the radio for Jacob's firefighting crew to handle a small fire that had broken out in a downtown apartment building. They hustled as always to make it in record time. But even in the few minutes it took them to weave through the afternoon traffic, the small fire had grown to engulf the entire building. "It was already looking pretty hopeless when we got there," says Jacob. "But luckily most of the people were already out."

By the time the twenty-four-year-old fireman arrived on the scene most of the hundred or so residents had already made it out of the blazing seven-story inferno.

But the firefighters had to be sure everyone was safe. So Jacob and his partners hurriedly entered the building clad in their fire-retardant gear, busting down doors and checking for any remaining trapped tenants. "It was a real old building in pretty bad shape," recalls Jacob. "Whole floors were crumbling faster than we could even get to them."

The roaring fire had started on the fifth floor before spreading throughout the rest of the building. Ladders enabled the firefighters to rescue residents on the top floors, but the fifth floor was too far gone to risk entering. They heard no screams or sounds, but they had no way of knowing without a physical check if there was anyone left on the fifth floor clinging to life. "It was unreasonable for any firefighters to enter the fifth floor at that point," says Jacob, "especially since everyone was already out of the building. But I had a nagging feeling that there was someone left." Finally ground personnel, who were busy taking names and trying to account for everyone in the building, radioed the order to evacuate. "It was way past the point of recklessness to be in there," recalls Jacob. "And they assured us everyone was out."

But suddenly, as Jacob and his colleagues came out of the front of the building, a young, frantic woman came running up to them yelling at the top of her lungs, "My baby, where is my Kris?" Remembers Jacob, "She was really hysterical, and she was running so fast she got past the barricade and almost knocked me down trying to get into the building." Jacob's instincts had been correct. The woman who lived in apartment 529 explained that she had left her seven-year-old son, Kris, alone for just a few minutes while she went down the street for some groceries. And ground personnel could not account for Kris anywhere. "I knew he was still in there," says Jacob. "I could just feel it. And the fact that I hadn't heard him screaming or calling out signaled to me he was either in shock or had passed out due to smoke inhalation. Either way I knew we didn't have time to waste."

Jacob and another firefighter made their way back up to the fifth floor while firefighters outside used ladders to look for any signs of life. Thick black smoke poured out of the windows and through the hallways, making it impossible to see anything inside the building or any-where near it. The heat inside had become so intense it was beginning to make the firefighters' protective cloth-ing almost unbearable.

By the time Jacob and his partner made it up to the fifth floor the roaring fire had grown so fierce, neither could see more than a few feet in front of them. Apart-ment 529 was engulfed in flames at the other end of the hall, and most of the floor was already impassable. "My partner looked at me and gave me the thumbs-down," explains Jacob. "As a fireman I knew he was right. The chances of us surviving if we went down that hall were slim, let alone anyone finding that boy. I had been in situations like that before where I had to accept the loss and I dealt with it. But I just kept seeing that mother's face in my head." For a moment Jacob's thoughts went to his own mother, who had died just a year earlier from cancer. "I guess for a split second I thought of how much my mom loved me so much all her life, and I just couldn't walk away from this one."

Suddenly Jacob darted down the hall without his partner, disappearing into the flames to find the missing boy. "It was weird because the instant I made the decision to run down that hallway a second later it seemed I was in front of the door, and it was already ajar."

As flames shot out of the apartment like fireballs he could see a little boy lying on the floor in just about the only spot that wasn't on fire. "I didn't even have time to figure out if he was alive or dead," says Jacob. "I just grabbed him and rushed out." Jacob and the boy cleared the fifth floor landing just as the fireman could hear the sound of the floor above crumbling.

Suddenly the tense crowd below broke into cheers as they saw Jacob emerge from the building with the boy. With Kris pressed up against his chest, Jacob could feel the boy's heart pounding, and when he coughed from the smoke, Jacob knew Kris would survive. Paramedics tended to the boy while Jacob himself collapsed. Jacob was a hero, but little did he know how his unselfish decision on that memorable day would affect his own life some twenty years later.

Two weeks after the rescue Jacob had two visitors appear at the station—Kris and his mother, Maria. They had come to thank him and told him they were forever in his debt. "They said they would repay me a life," says Jacob. "I was pretty stunned. I remember I didn't know what to say. But I went along with it. I figured they would forget about me." But Kris and Maria never forgot. Maria made sure her son visited Jacob at least one day every week after school. "He would bring me a lunch from his mom or a candy bar, just something to say thanks," recalls Jacob. "But he did it just about every week, which amazed me. He didn't have a father so I guess I kind of became a good influence on his life as well. After a few months we really became friends."

As the years went on Kris continued his weekly visits. By this time the two were spending time with each other outside of work as well. "I used to take him to Cubs games and to a movie every once in a while," says Jacob. "He was always a great kid."

A few years later Jacob married, started his own family and left the fire department to start his own insurance company. Kris joined the Army, then went to college, but the two remained in touch, writing letters and talking on the telephone, and still taking in a Cubs game at least once a year. Kris eventually graduated from college and became a teacher.

Unfortunately, at age thirty-seven, Jacob was diagnosed with diabetes. And despite treatments and diet, the disease began to deteriorate his kidneys until he was diagnosed with end-stage kidney failure at the age of forty-three. With two children in high school and his wife pregnant with a third, it was not a good situation. "I was really devastated," reveals Jacob. "I'd saved a lot of people in my years as a firefighter and after that I was a pretty good husband and provider. But for the first time in my life I was really scared, and I didn't know what to do."

With no brothers or sisters and his wife the wrong blood type, Jacob was forced to depend on a donor kidney from the bank of available kidneys at a time when donorship was not yet at the level it is today. "I really didn't know where to turn. That's when I got Kris's call."

It was time for Kris and Jacob to take in their yearly baseball game, and so, expecting a day at the park, Kris called only to hear that Jacob was on his deathbed. "I answered the phone and I remember I didn't want to tell Kris what happened. But my wife said it would be wrong to keep it from him. I barely got the words out when he asked me what my blood type was. I told him, and he said he'd call me right back."

As Kris contemplated his friend's unfortunate situation, his thoughts kept returning to that fateful moment years earlier when he looked up and saw his hero Jacob's face as he carried Kris out of the burning building. He knew had it not been for Jacob, he would not be alive today. No matter how he thought about it, Kris just kept coming to one conclusion—Jacob had saved his life. Now Kris could finally repay the favor. He knew what he had to do.

Within an hour Kris was at Jacob's doorstep with a lifesaving message. "He comes to the door and says, 'It's your lucky day, I'm the same blood type, and I'll bail you out of this one,'" remembers Jacob. "So I say to him, 'You'll do what?' I was really in shock—and he says, 'I've got two kidneys, and you can have one.'"

At first Jacob resisted putting his young friend through the trauma of having a kidney removed. But when medical tests confirmed Kris would be the perfect donor and with time running out, Jacob accepted his incredibly generous offer. "I really had nowhere else to turn. And he was determined that I accept his offer. He told me he loved me like a father and it was the least he could do for me."

On a cold winter's day in January 1994, Jacob and Kris entered the hospital escorted by their loving wives. The operation was a perfect success.

Today both Jacob and Kris are living happy and healthy lives in Chicago. Kris is now an English teacher. Jacob, retired, volunteers his time as a counselor for inner-city programs for underprivileged children. And best of all, Jacob and Kris still go to a Cubs game every year.

"Jacob says we're even now," says Kris. "But the truth is he was there all my life to help me make decisions and give me guidance and support. I'm just glad there was something I could do to pay him back for saving my life."

A Badge of Love

*J*oe was a career cop who thought he'd seen it, heard it and done it all when it came to working the streets. So when he took a job with the Los Angeles Police Department in December 1982, he had no idea it would change his life forever. Over fifteen years of police work on the east coast of the United States had hardened him. The violent streets of inner-city Los Angeles were no trouble for the gruff and tough thirty-seven-year-old lawman. "I was pretty cynical," says Joe. "I thought everybody was doing something wrong, it was just a matter of catching them at it, especially these street punks I had to deal with."

For decades, the gang-infested streets of Los Angeles

had witnessed needless bloodshed, and most LAPD cops considered their job like a tour of duty in a war zone. "When you hit the streets each morning, you just had one wish, 'Please God don't let me die today,' " recalls Joe. "And 'Let me get them before they get me.' Nobody would admit to an outsider that we thought like that, but we did!"

It was on one such ordinary deadly day when Joe would cross paths with a local seventeen-year-old street kid named Sam. The son of an Alabama preacher, Sam's mother and father had recently been killed in an auto accident back home, and Sam had just moved in with his widowed aunt in Los Angeles. He wanted so much to be like his dad, but with no friends or protectors, it was a tough road to travel. "My pop was an amazing man who taught me to love, but he also taught me to fight to survive," says Sam. "When I moved to L.A., I was all alone. If I didn't join up with a gang, I'd be dead."

The neighborhood gangs pressured Sam into crime and violence as soon as he arrived, and it wasn't long before he started to get into trouble. A few days after moving in he got into his first gang fight, which left one dead and several of his gang brothers wounded. And only a few weeks later he was stealing cars and selling drugs, and even drove the getaway car for a liquor store robbery that ended in a bloody shoot-out between gang members and the police.

But still Sam tried as hard as he could to make a difference. In the short time he'd been in town he was already known by his gang friends as P, a reference to his preacher father, his booming voice and his constant fearless attempts to convince his gang brothers that they should be fighting *for* each other instead of against each other. He constantly risked his life defying gang leaders, refusing to fire a gun or even carry one and threatening anyone who sold drugs to kids. He even convinced some of his hoodlum friends to help organize a football team for the neighborhood kids. He was trying to be a ray of hope in the sea of despair and that's how he met Joe.

Joe and his partner were patrolling a crime-ridden area in L.A. one day when they spotted a few well-known gang kids harassing schoolkids. "They were trying to jack these kids—make them give up their money or try and sell some drugs," recalls Joe. The two officers stayed back for a moment to see if they could observe a crime being committed and make an arrest. After witnessing one of the hoodlums reach into a child's pockets and take his money, they were ready to move in and make their bust.

But seconds before they approached, they suddenly saw Sam emerge from out of nowhere and rip the money from the thug's hand. Assuming he was another gang member, they stayed back waiting to see if he too would commit a crime. "Me and my partner both thought this was just another wiseguy chiming in on the action, who wanted the money, so we hung out for a second." But to the contrary, the teen was about to risk his life to help the young child. "All of a sudden this smart-ass-looking scrappy kid starts smacking these tough guys around, not punching or anything but just telling them off and shoving them. I thought he was a gang leader or something but then I saw something I'd never seen before in all my years as a cop." As the officers watched they saw the tough-as-nails gang members suddenly run away and Sam return the stolen money. "Both my partner and I were completely dumbfounded. We immediately approached him to find out what was up. Our first thought was that this had to be a new gang leader but why he did what he did just really didn't add up."

As the officers approached, they prepared for a chase, thinking Sam would run, but as they abruptly pulled their squad car up alongside him, he didn't move. "We really expected to chase him down," admits Joe. "But when he didn't run we were amazed. We knew there was something different about this kid."

The officers soon found out Sam was indeed like no other. "He had no fear," remembers Joe. "But when we told him to freeze and tell us what he was doing, he very carefully and calmly told us he was watching out for the kids." Even though Sam was a gang member and agreed to go along with his hoodlum friends on local heists and gang warfare, he absolutely drew the line when fellow members tried to ruin the lives of the neighborhood's young children. "I did what I had to do to survive," says Sam. "But I wasn't going to let them hurt these kids. I knew that was wrong. I can't explain why it made such a difference to me even then. It just did."

Sam sparked something in Joe's heart. "It got to me," reveals Joe. "I know it probably sounds ridiculous coming from a guy like me, but I just got this warm feeling inside. I really felt this kid was different, you know, like he had compassion. I thought he might have a chance to turn his life around and really help others." The thrice-divorced and childless cop was hardly a pushover. He had all but given up on the human race. In fact, Joe had been brought up before disciplinary boards several times for being a little too rough in other cities. And he was already getting into trouble in L.A. for being verbally abusive when questioning people.

But something in the way Sam stood up for those young kids melted the aging officer's heart. "I had seen so much death and cruelty between people out there in the streets. I'd seen parents kill their own kids, brothers raping sisters, and the worst of life. It was a godsend for me to see someone who had such compassion in his heart even though he was in the middle of all that crap."

Over the next six months, the two got to know each other, and Joe became Sam's unofficial protector. Joe was always sure to make at least one run a day by Sam's aunt's house, and the two played basketball together on the weekends from time to time at the local YMCA. Joe began taking a great interest in Sam's future. He found out that Sam, who was to graduate from high school that year, wanted to go to college but didn't have the money. "His parents never had any life insurance or anything," explains Joe. "He was able to get a little financial aid but no way was it enough to move out of that neighborhood and get a place and pay tuition."

Meanwhile, Joe knew all too well that Sam, who was still deeply entrenched in the gang lifestyle of stealing, fighting and dealing drugs, was headed straight for prison. But Joe was convinced that if he just kept the lines of communication between them open, he could perhaps help Sam change.

That change came sooner than he thought when Sam's gang brothers gave him a life-or-death ultimatum. "They told me to lose the cop or they were going to kill me," says Sam. "And I knew they were serious."

Sam told Joe he could no longer hang out with him, and that Joe should leave him alone. "I knew something was wrong when he tried to blow me off," says Joe. "We had become good friends. And I knew he was really scared about something, but he wouldn't tell me what. I knew it had to be the boys that were threatening him; it was the only logical reason for him to say what he said."

Joe immediately felt compelled to help. "I knew the only answer was to get him out of that neighborhood quick and get him into college," says Joe. "That way he would have a future and an escape." Joe explained to Sam how he could leave school early and take his GED high school equivalency test. Then he could immediately go to college. Sam was open to the idea, but where would he get the money? "I checked out every single scholarship program plus all the financial aid stuff," says Joe. "But it all took so long and we didn't have time. We needed to get him out of the neighborhood right away and in college the next semester." Joe spent almost every hour he wasn't working researching how he could get Sam into college and get him the money he needed quickly.

Finally the answer came to Joe—he would foot the bill. "It hit me all of a sudden," recalls Joe. "Why don't I just pay his tuition and rent and get him out of there? I became a cop initially to help people and stop crime. Well, here was my chance. And I swear I loved this kid like a son anyway."

Sam was floored when Joe told him the news. No one had ever done anything like this for him. "My dad always told me to believe and have faith," says Sam. "Joe made me believe that my dad was right. When I lost my parents, I felt like I lost everything in the world. But Joe was giving me my life back. My whole life changed right there."

Sam passed his GED and started classes two months later during the spring semester at UCLA. He rented a small apartment and roomed with three other guys. It was worlds away from the ghetto. He declared his major in criminal justice. "I thought he was just majoring in that because he thought he owed it to me," says Joe, "me being a cop and all that. So I told him he could be whatever he wanted. That's when he told me he decided he wanted to be a lawyer. I couldn't believe it. I always wanted to be a lawyer, but I never had the grades for it myself."

For the next three years Joe continued to pay about half of all Sam's bills through undergraduate classes, and the two friends grew even closer, continuing to play basketball together on weekends and seeing each other whenever they could. Sam excelled at school, graduating with a 3.4 grade point average and earning a full-ride scholarship to Harvard Law School.

Three years after he graduated, Sam returned to his old neighborhood, where he became an activist working with a private nonprofit community group to get hardcore criminals off the streets and away from the kids in the ghettos. "It's my way of doing what Joe said he always wanted to do—help people and help society," says Sam. "If I can save one kid, then that kid could turn around and save ten or one hundred people down the line. There's no better reward than that. And no better way to show my gratitude for Joe."

Joe, who has long since retired from the force and now runs his own delicatessen, believes that Sam has accomplished more than he could ever have hoped for. Sam even convinced the once-hard-hearted Joe to become a volunteer with a local inner-city youth program. "He always tells me that I saved his life," says Joe. "That's true, but he saved my heart. And for a bastard like me that's a real miracle.

"I never had a son, but Sam has loved and respected me like a father, and there's no sign of love that could make this father more proud than to see what Sam is doing with his life. He's made me the happiest man on earth."

A Stranger's Gift

~~~

Marilyn was thirty-three years old. Her fiancé had just dumped her, she lost her job as an accountant, her landlord raised her rent and her car blew its transmission—all on the same day. "It was just too much," remembers Marilyn. "I couldn't believe how my whole life could just fall apart like that so quickly. I was devastated."

Still wearing her gray suit from work, Marilyn boarded a midtown Manhattan bus at five P.M. to take her back home to her now unaffordable apartment. In her mind, she kept replaying the scene of her boss eloquently explaining to her that her dismissal was nothing personal, "just a matter of cutbacks and all that."

She fought to hold back the tears as she stared out the window at the lights of New York and remembered how she used to gaze out at those same lights with the man she loved—who now was in love with someone else. The beauty of the cityscape was lost on her, and soon the tears streamed down her flushed cheeks. What on earth am I going to do with my life now? she thought over and over. Where will I go? Lost in her own thoughts, she was unaware of the dashing businessman staring at her from across the aisle.

She sobbed quietly the whole way home, only occasionally stopping to blow her nose with a tissue she took from her purse. As the bus neared her stop, she rose and walked to the door right next to where the businessman was seated, barely noticing how nicely dressed he was. When the bus stopped, Marilyn got off and briskly walked the one block to her apartment, hoping to reach home before the fast-approaching darkness. Upon arriving she walked into her apartment, turned on the light and locked the door behind her, just like she had done a million times before.

As she threw her purse on the couch she noticed a small envelope sticking out of the outside pocket. "I knew I didn't put that there," recalls Marilyn. "And it worried me a little." She slowly opened up the mysterious envelope to find a letter. The greeting read, "From the gentleman on the bus." Marilyn sat down in shock.

"Dear Loved Lady," the note began. "Please don't cry. Be happy! Today I was given the gift of life, and I want to share a little of it with you."

The unusual and unexpected note explained how the man had just come from the hospital where he was told a spot on his lungs wasn't cancerous. Before his appointment, he explained, he had spent the entire afternoon walking the streets of Manhattan thinking of all the things he would still be able to do even if he did have cancer, and even if he was dying. "I don't know what you are crying about," his note continued, "but as long as you can feel the breeze blowing through your beautiful hair, then please cherish it. Listen to the birds serenade you while you can. Blush when a handsome man flirts with you. And do something nice for someone who needs a little helping hand, out of love and for no other reason. I guarantee you, no matter how bad things are, you'll feel better!" It was signed, "Just Someone Who Cares."

Marilyn stopped crying, went to the kitchen and opened up the refrigerator door, took out a carton of ice cream, and then she picked up the phone to call an old friend to say hello. "I thought I lost everything that day, including the only man I ever loved," says Marilyn. "But just then I felt as if the whole world was in love with me! I realized that a total stranger had just changed my whole outlook on life! Life is full of surprises."

The Love Bug

⟳

*T*anya was up to her eyeballs in problems. The twenty-two-year-old single mother of three young boys was doing her best to deal with a deadbeat ex-husband who had left her and her kids with nothing but debts. Her job as a customer service representative for a local wireless telephone company in Atlanta, Georgia, didn't even come close to paying the bills, so she worked two other jobs: as a delivery driver for a newspaper distribution company and as an errand runner for a local messenger service.

She was doing all she could to keep her children eating and unaware of how desperate their situation really was. And to make matters worse her widowed mom was in the hospital dying of cancer, and her Social Security and Medicare benefits weren't covering all the treatments.

But it was the day when her old station wagon's engine blew up while taking her kids to school that Tanya had finally had all she could take. "It was a catastrophe," remembers Tanya. "There was no way I could afford another car or even to fix that one. I was dead broke." She was already behind on all of her bills, including the rent on her family's one-bedroom apartment. And she needed the car for work. Without it she would lose two of her jobs, which would put her and her children on the street for sure. "I was trying so hard to hang on to what we had," says Tanya. "But I just couldn't handle this."

Despite all her problems, Tanya was a proud woman who was trying to pick herself up and make a go of life. But now her faith was really being tested. Her husband had maxed out the one credit card the couple had before he left, and she didn't have a dime of savings left.

As she sat there on the roadway with the engine smoking and her three boys screaming at the top of their lungs in frustration, she broke down and cried. "I swear I just wished I could close my eyes, go to sleep and never wake up again," reveals Tanya. "It was all too much for me to take. I didn't know how to go on anymore."

Tanya didn't even have the money to get a tow truck to get her car off the road. And as the highway patrolmen pulled up to assist her, she didn't know what she was going to tell them to do with the car. "They told me I had twenty minutes to get the car off the road or they were going to impound it," remembers Tanya. "I had no way of paying to get that car out of an impound or get it towed out of there to a shop, and I couldn't afford to get it fixed. So I just said do what you want with it." Tanya and her children took all their belongings out of the car and waved good-bye as the police tow truck towed their only means of transportation away.

As she stood with her children on the side of the road, crying and arguing with the police, an elegant stranger pulled up in a new Volkswagen Bug. The driver, Sally, had been a bit of a hell-raiser in her day, protesting for the American Civil Liberties Union. Now the childless seventy-two-year-old retired real estate agent was feeling old, useless and lonely after the recent loss of her husband.

Sally was driving back from a routine checkup at her doctor's office when she spotted Tanya and her children on the side of the road. "I was surprised nobody else had pulled over yet to help her," says Sally. "It was shocking that the sight of a young mother with all those kids on the side of the road wouldn't attract more help than just me."

As the police argued with Tanya, who was refusing to allow them to drive her home, Sally casually sauntered up to Tanya's side wearing a big sunhat and shades as if she were Tanya's best buddy picking her up for a day at the beach. Tanya remembers, "I was hysterical when all of a sudden this funny, sweet-looking lady appears out of nowhere and tells me she's here to help. I thought she was a nut at first."

When the police officer asked if Tanya knew Sally, the eccentric lady pulled Tanya aside and asked her what the problem was. "I figured I had nothing to lose at that point," says Tanya. "I started telling her the whole story."

Tanya began to explain her dilemma to Sally, but she was still hysterical and not much was getting through the sobbing. "I was pretty upset," remembers Tanya. "I think all that I could explain was that we had lost our car and didn't want to go with the police."

Sally offered Tanya and her children a ride home in her Bug and they accepted. After they started driving, Sally calmed Tanya down enough to find out the rest of her story. "I felt like I could talk to her right away," remembers Tanya. "She was like a mother who really seemed to care about what I was going through. And she was listening when nobody else I knew would. I realized talking wasn't going to make my problems go away, but it was nice to get all that off my chest."

The two became fast friends on the ride home and soon Sally was sharing her life story with Tanya, starting with how depressed she was about her husband recently dying. She told the young mother how impressed she was with what Tanya was trying to accomplish for her children and how she had always wished for children herself. Then Sally started to cry. "Her crying stopped me from crying," remembers Tanya, "and now *I* was trying to calm *her* down. It was like a soap opera. Then my one-year-old joined in crying too, and of course me and Sally had to laugh."

Tanya really felt like she had found someone special. As she was reaching in her purse to get a pen and paper out to exchange phone numbers with Sally they neared her building, but Sally failed to stop and buzzed right by Tanya's apartment. "I figured she just missed it," remembers Tanya, "So I politely mentioned that she passed my place. But she didn't say anything."

Sally didn't turn around but instead pushed her foot down on the accelerator and headed back toward the freeway. When Tanya frantically asked her where she was going, Sally calmly told her it was a surprise. "I started to worry about my kids," says Tanya. "I could tell she was harmless and sweet, but I thought maybe she could be a little wacky or something, and I didn't want us in a car with someone like that."

After a few minutes Sally pulled off the freeway and drove the Bug through the gates of one of the city's most exclusive developments. While Tanya sat stunned and confused, her children marveled at the big, beautiful houses. Then Sally pulled into the drive of one of the palatial estates and parked. "I still wasn't scared," remembers Tanya. "But I was angry because I figured this woman was nuts and now we were going to have to get out and wind up paying for an even more expensive cab ride home than from the freeway."

When an angry Tanya again asked Sally what she thought she was doing, Sally sent her into shock when she told Tanya to take the car and go home. "I didn't know what to say," remembers Tanya. "I thought I was on *Candid Camera* or something. But she said it again and she was serious."

As it turned out, the house belonged to Sally, and she wanted Tanya to have the car, to help her out. Her only request was that she wanted the two to become friends. But Tanya was still skeptical until Sally leaned over and took the registration out of the glove compartment and signed it over to her.

"I wanted to be her friend anyway, but I couldn't take her car," says Tanya, who turned down the expensive gift. "I told her that she didn't need to give me a car for me to be her friend." But Sally wouldn't take no for an answer. She put the keys in Tanya's hands and insisted that if she was her friend, then she would accept the gift or else she would break her heart. Only then did Tanya finally accept.

"I was so happy I threw my arms around her and

wouldn't let go," says Tanya. "This was a huge miracle for me. She made me the happiest person on earth. I still can't believe it really happened."

Tanya took the car home, and the two women became close friends over the next few years. With Sally's continued support and advice Tanya succeeded in pulling herself out of her financial troubles and was eventually able to get a much better paying job. Meanwhile, Sally became like a grandmother to Tanya's children, deriving countless hours of joy from their company. After Tanya's mother passed away a year later, Sally became like a second mom to her.

"Tanya had lost so much that I was overjoyed to help her get a little bit back," says Sally. "And she gave me something I never had—a family. We helped each other, and that's what life is really all about."

The Bottom Line

*N*ate was terrified he was going to lose his print-
ing business. He was in the middle of a bidding
war for a big print campaign for one of the area's hottest
telecommunications companies, and if he got the account, it could mean millions to his company in the long
run. The only problem was his company was so small,
and even for the chance of winning the contract couldn't
afford to outbid bigger companies who had better cash
reserves and could absorb more cost than him. So he cut
the salaries of his entire twelve-person staff by 20 percent, sending his employees into a panic.

The thirty-two-year-old Miami native explained to his
loyal workers who had all been with him since he started

three years earlier that he needed to beat the competition. And cutting salaries was the only way to do it. "I tried telling them that this was for their own good in the long run," remembers Nate. "But it didn't really go over too well."

Nate went crazy trying to think of ways to cut costs on materials, machinery and finally people in order to deliver a competitive price. "This job would really put me on the map," says Nate. "It would bring in a whole lot more business in the future." Nate became so obsessed with getting the contract, he couldn't sleep, couldn't eat and all his employees now hated him. What's more, he wasn't even going to make any money on the project if he did get it, since the bids were already well below his profit margin. But he wouldn't give up. "I was so desperate for success," says Nate. "I didn't care what it took to get this job. I convinced myself this was the only way for me to grow."

And while Nate became Captain Bly, his frustrated employees stuck by him, despite his abuse and the harsh pay cuts. Every day they suggested ideas on how to bring in more jobs or work the presses more efficiently. Then one day his foreman came to him and told him he'd solved his bid problems. "He told me to bow out of the bidding war," remembers Nate. "He said I was killing myself and the company by trying too hard for this one." Nate was so irate with what he thought was "giving up" he almost fired him on the spot.

As Nate racked his brain day and night trying to figure out how to get the prized contract, his foreman was putting together a campaign that would blow Nate's mind and force him to reevaluate everything he thought he knew about business. The day before Nate was scheduled to submit his proposal and bid, he sat despondently in his office, going over the unfavorable numbers again and again in his head. He could get the job, but his bid would be so low he would have to take out loans just to keep his company going until the anticipated increase in revenue from the exposure came in. He thought it was worth it, but it was a very high price to pay.

While Nate labored over the proposal, his foreman walked in, followed by Nate's entire staff. Nate expected a mutiny and figured they were all going to quit at the same time. But contrary to Nate's fear, they came ready to bail him out. They had spent the last month formulating an alternative business plan for Nate, which didn't require the telecommunications contract he was killing himself over. And their plan would save the salaries that his employees' families depended on.

Their plan was sweet and simple. "Give and you shall receive!" explains Nate. "That was their proposal." They pointed out to the upstart owner that if he took the same loss he was planning to take but spent the money on their salaries, he would get a whole lot more bang for his buck. In exchange for restoring their normal salaries, the employees would all bring in at least one paying client and maybe more. Plus they all had contacts in the social services sectors that they knew would bring in more business. "It was an interesting idea," says Nate. "But it was a huge gamble." When Nate looked unconvinced, his employees all told him they would voluntarily take a whopping 50 percent pay cut if their plan didn't pan out within six months. "They really believed in this," says Nate. "And they wanted to make it work. Then they all told me they loved me. That was the clincher. Something came over me and I took a chance."

Within three months Nate's company and name were all over the city, and before long he was getting more business than he could handle. On top of that, the publicity he garnered for his positive program earned him several local awards and even more contracts. He then gave all his employees a 25 percent increase over their original pay.

Nate's business grew by leaps and bounds until he sold it for an enormous profit four years later. But more than the money, he'll never forget the valuable lesson he learned. "You get what you give," says Nate, "plus a whole lot more!"

A Father's Promise

$\backsim$

$\mathcal{E}$arly one blustery winter morning, two Alaskan hunters set out from their village for a day of fishing and caribou hunting. Morris and Sayer had grown up together in Point Hope, Alaska, a tiny community of about five hundred people more than three hundred miles north of the Arctic Circle. The remote village can only be reached by plane or boat, and little has changed there in the last hundred years. "Most of us survive on hunting," says Sayer. "Polar bears, caribou and stuff like that. It's our way of life, so we don't think twice about going out into the cold and snow because we have to do it to eat."

The lifelong pals, both in their fifties, were top-notch

hunters who had learned the ways of their elders. Like their fathers before them, the experienced Eskimos had deep respect for the treacherous terrain they faced every time they ventured out into the desolate wilderness. "You have to learn early that the country here is very dangerous," explains Sayer. "The elements like the cold and water can get you so fast. We have seen many people die out there over the years."

Morris and Sayer mounted their snowmobiles with their sleds in tow and headed forty miles into the mountains for a day of hunting, just like they had done a thousand times before.

After a successful day of hunting, they noticed the sun was setting, and knew they needed to start back before temperatures plunged, turning the winter wonderland before them into a frozen desert. So the two friends headed their snowmobiles toward home with the day's kill tied to their sleds. But the blowing winter winds had changed the lay of the land since the men had set out that morning. Confused by the drifting snow, they soon veered off course. The gentle hum of their snowmobiles was abruptly interrupted by the alarming sound of cracking ice, and Morris felt the ground below him give way. In the blink of an eye, he was sucked into the frigid water of a giant lake.

Before Morris even knew what was happening his friend Sayer also came crashing through the ice. With both snowmobiles lost, the two men were submerged in the deadly water and swimming for their lives. "The moment I hit the water, I could feel it come inside my clothes," says Morris. "It actually felt warm at first." The 25-degree water felt comforting to Morris compared to the frigid below-zero temperature outside. But that comfortable sensation wouldn't last long. Sayer, who popped to the surface close to the edge of the ice, quickly lifted himself out of the deadly water. But after pulling himself up on the ice, he looked back and saw his friend Morris had drifted far out into the lake.

"He was way out there," says Sayer. "I can't say just how far, but I knew it was too far for him to swim back in on his own. It looked like all he could do was hang on." Morris was struggling to stay afloat by paddling furiously with his arms. Then he saw his sled pop up from below the surface. "I couldn't make it back to the shore," says Morris, "but when I saw my sled I swam over to it." Weighed down by heavy clothes, he was barely able to float even with the help of his sled. And the warm feeling the water gave him at first had quickly changed into numbing cold.

Morris and Sayer both knew that death comes quickly in water that cold. Sayer frantically searched for a branch or a log, anything he could use to paddle over to save his friend. But the barren winter landscape offered nothing. Yet, determined to help Morris, Sayer did the unimaginable and leaped back into the deadly water. "It was so cold, I started cramping up the second I got in," remembers Sayer. "I knew I could never make it out to him and survive." Sayer quickly jumped back out of the water, drenched and painfully aware he was unable to help his friend. "When I finally realized I could do nothing, I became very upset," says Sayer. "I didn't want to leave him."

As Morris looked back to the shore, he saw his friend paralyzed with fear, and he knew what that meant. Realizing Sayer held his life in his hands, he quickly yelled to his pal to snap him out of his depressed state. " 'Hey bro, what are you crying for?' I screamed at him as loud as I could," says Morris. " 'I'm not dead yet.' " The shout brought Sayer back to reality, and that's when he made the difficult decision to leave his friend and make the almost-impossible journey back to the village on foot to get help. But as Sayer turned his back toward Morris and headed off, both men knew he might never make it back in time. After all, most doctors agree that after a half hour in water that cold the chances of survival are slim to none. Morris called out to his friend one last time with a message for his children, who had lost their mother years earlier in an auto accident. "Just tell my kids I love them all very much," Morris screamed out with as much strength as he could muster. Those words cut through Sayer's freezing chest like a knife. "I thought those might be the last words I heard from him," remembers Sayer.

As Sayer headed back to the village across the blurry frozen land, Morris knew he must try and do the impossible and hang on until help came. The devoted father of four quickly began concentrating on the love he had for his children. They had never really recovered from the loss of their mother after she was killed instantly in a head-on collision with another vehicle, and he couldn't bear the thought of leaving them orphans. He couldn't leave them. He wouldn't! " 'Is my daughter gonna come home and find out she has a dead father?' I kept saying to myself," says Morris. " 'No!' I told myself. 'No!' I kept thinking of her face the night before when she told me to be safe, like she always did since her mother died. And how I promised her I'd come home just fine. I told her how much I loved her. And that gave me strength to keep going and fight the cold. I couldn't let her or the rest of my kids down."

Meanwhile Sayer was faced with his own life-and-death struggle as he made the ten-mile journey back to Point Hope soaking wet and already frozen. "I could already begin to feel my body stiffen from hypothermia as soon as I started," says Sayer. "And I was getting weaker and weaker fast. But I knew my friend would die if I didn't get back fast so I kept going." Sayer had his own wife and eight children to think of as well.

As night fell on the frozen tundra, Sayer was beginning to stumble, exhaustion taking its toll on the devoted friend. Each time he fell it was that much harder to pick himself up. "By that time, it would take me four or five minutes to get up after one of those falls," recalls Sayer. "My body was cramping up bad by the fourth or fifth mile. There were so many things going through my mind. It was like I was having nightmares or something. But I just kept concentrating on saving my friend. I knew if I fell down one more time, that I probably would not be able to get back up."

The weakened Sayer soon began walking backward with the wind at his face because it stopped him from stumbling. "I just took one step at a time backwards like that," recalls Sayer, "trying to keep believing that I could make it, and that I could help my friend." Then, as if it were a dream, Sayer suddenly saw the lights of the city up ahead. Nearly four hours after setting out on his journey he had made it back. Minutes later a rescue party was on its way to find Morris. And incredibly, he was still alive!

"All of a sudden I heard something in the water and it sounded like a boat," remembers Morris. "At first I thought I was hallucinating; then I passed out. I began dreaming about my kids and how I promised my daughter I'd return. I just kept thinking even in my dream of how much I loved them all." The rescuers scrambled to pry his frozen hands from the sled and pull him from the water, then rushed him back to the village where an emergency helicopter waited to fly him almost two hundred miles to the nearest hospital. When he arrived in the emergency room Morris's body temperature was only 75 degrees, which meant severe hypothermia had set in. By any medical standard it was a miracle he was alive. "Normally people don't live long in water that cold," recalled the attending ER doctor. "At thirty minutes, you can usually start to do a countdown. After everything he went through, he really should have been dead about an hour after he went into the water, at the latest. Morris lasted a lot longer than that. And medically I'm at a loss to explain why."

But Morris insists he knows exactly what kept him alive—the powerful love he had for his children, whom he had promised he would come home to.

"I wasn't going to let my kids down and allow them to become orphans. I love them so much. That's where I got my strength," says Morris. "That was my turning point. That's why I survived while another man might not have." But he also knows that his love and devotion to his children wouldn't have meant a thing if it wasn't for the death-defying love of his friend Sayer. "If I could ever do anything like that for him ever I would do it without any question," says Morris. "I'll help him anyplace, anytime he needs me. No matter what, for the rest of my life."

Drunk with Love

⁓

*C*arl was a Methodist minister who wanted more than anything to preach God's word from the time he was a child. Growing up in West Texas, Carl was the son of ultra-strict immigrant parents who were long on discipline and short on love. Things were so strict that he had never even tasted alcohol until he was thirty years old, but one sip and he fell in love with booze. "I was immediately hooked," says Carl. "Like most addicts I was trying to numb the pain. I had a very cold childhood with a rigid upbringing, and drinking was my way of getting over that."

Amazingly, Carl became an alcoholic within only weeks after taking his first taste of alcohol and soon was polishing off a fifth of bourbon a day. It ruined his life quicker than he could ever have imagined. He was forced to give up his position in the church and became a teacher in order to try and make a living. "You cannot be a minister and alcoholic at the same time," says Carl. "It just doesn't work. So I just quit preaching because I could not stop drinking. I had to make a choice, and I chose booze."

For the next two decades, Carl became more and more addicted to alcohol, sinking deeper and deeper into depression as his dependence grew. It was wrecking his marriage, and while he was now a professor of Family Studies at Texas Tech University, even his teaching career was finally in jeopardy. "Drinking was everything to me," explains Carl. "I really no longer cared about anything or anyone else that got in the way of that bottle. I'd have my first drink about mid-morning at the office, then more at lunch, then continue right into the afternoon. Then I'd go home and drink till I was numbed up."

His drinking became so obsessive, he reached a point where he didn't even care where he was when he drank or who he was around. "I would drink at home, at the office, in the car, in the garage and everywhere," recalls Carl. "I really didn't care if my kids were watching or my wife. People at school knew I was neglecting my classes and my duties, and I wasn't there for students. But I really didn't care as long as I had that drink."

Though he managed to make enough excuses for himself to hold on to his job, he was completely destroying his marriage and his children's future, and he was in desperate financial trouble. Drinking was expensive. "I had become pretty neglectful and abusive with my family," admits Carl. "I was mean and really unreachable. The bills were totally out of control. And I used to sit there right in front of my kids and get drunk. I knew it was just a matter of time before my wife left me."

With everything he ever cared about now slipping through his fingers and no hope for the future, he didn't care if he lived or died. "I had nowhere else to turn," remembers Carl. "I had become a bad teacher, a bad husband and father. I thought I was just too far gone to come back."

So the former minister decided to commit suicide. He resolved that since he was slowly killing himself with his habit, he might as well end things quickly and spare his wife and children a lifetime of misery. He planned on being dead before Christmas of that year.

But then just weeks before he would have ended it all, an old friend suddenly reappeared out of nowhere and changed everything. "I didn't even know he knew I was an alcoholic," says Carl. "But he let me know that I wasn't hiding a thing from anyone. He loved me enough to tell it to me straight and he physically made me go to an AA meeting."

Over the course of the next few months his friend refused to give up on him. He convinced Carl that his life wasn't over and that there was still time for him to fix his world and be something special for the ones he loved. He assured Carl that he was there for him to lean on and convinced Carl to check himself into a full rehab program because he knew Carl was too far gone for any lesser measures. Says Carl, "I can't explain it but somehow knowing somebody was out there who knew all my secrets and still believed in me and cared enough to refuse to give up on me made all the difference."

The simple but unexplainable force of friendship was what Carl needed to get him back on his feet. Within six months he was sober and putting his life back together. "That was sixteen years ago," marvels Carl, "and I haven't had a drop of liquor since."

Carl longed to pay back the awesome favor that saved his life. But his friend refused to collect any debt from Carl, only requesting that he promise to reach out and help others the same way he was helped. Carl quickly realized that the best way he could help other addicts was to use his skills as an educator to teach them what he knew about addiction through his position at the university. So Carl single-handedly spearheaded the creation of the first college program in the world to help addicts get back on their feet and get educated at Texas Tech University. "So many recovering addicts are locked into lower sectors of society because they are uneducated and therefore don't have many opportunities," explains Carl. "I wanted to change that."

Since the Texas Tech Center for Addiction Studies started a little over four years ago, it has saved over six hundred lives. "We've made a doctor, three lawyers, teachers, accountants and even some drug counselors," Carl says proudly. "These former addicts are now very productive members of society all because there was a support system of knowledge and, most of all, friendship here at the university to guide them through healing. I know a lot of these people would have been dead if it wasn't for this program."

Carl is happy to have survived his own addiction and has rebuilt his marriage and his relationship with his children. And every day he is only too willing to be able to return the love and friendship that saved his life. "Because of my addiction, I was going to lose my wife, my family and everything that was important to me," says Carl. "I would have lost my life if someone didn't help me. Now I'm giving others the chance to save their lives."

Love Is Kid Stuff

The afternoon started off as a romp through the woods for twelve-year-old best friends John and Greg. "I'm a better climber than you," Greg, the muscled swimmer who had started weight lifting that summer, bragged to John as the two boys started out on their rock climbing expedition outside of Sedona, Arizona.

"No, you're not," protested John as he ran ahead. "I can climb better than you any day." They never told their parents they would be scaling the jagged cliffs of the red rock country, but they had grown up in these parts and were used to rugged terrain. Together they had played in rapids, hunted deer and climbed these mountains many a time without incident.

As the midday sun and 100-degree heat warmed the backs of their necks, the boys hiked their way two miles into the canyon until they gazed up at the ominous slick walls of the massive mountain before them. "Well, let's get to it," Greg called out to his pal John. "Let's synchronize our watches and we will rendezvous at Eagle Base at thirteen hundred hours."

Of course the boys weren't climbing to the top of the mammoth peak. The plan was to just venture up fifty feet or so to a perch where they had built a fort. They were bringing up supplies just as they had done each day for the last week. Today's haul was a flashlight, some dry cereal, water and survival gear their parents had bought them from a local army supply store. "Affirmative, Captain!" answered John.

The two boys fastened their backpacks and confidently forged up the mountain as they had done a hundred times before. "I'll go first," said Greg as he started out. But John protested. "No, you went first last time," he said. "I'll go." And up went John, wearing shorts and T-shirt, showing off his expensive hiking boots. Greg followed about ten feet below.

As they made their way up the mountain, the boys decided to take different routes to their destination. A few minutes after they split up, John was having a little trouble getting his footing, so he stuck his shoe into a deep crevice for support while he tried to lift himself to the next level. As John dug in deeper with his foot, suddenly he heard the all-too-familiar sound of a rattlesnake! As he jerked his foot away and screamed, the snake lunged at his bare leg and bit him. Greg was almost up to the fort and although he heard John scream, he couldn't see his friend. So he quickly worked his way around to the side of the mountain and tried to get a glimpse of John.

He was astonished to find John dangling with his backpack snagged on a sturdy branch growing out of a ledge ten feet below and about twenty feet to the left. The jolt from the bite had made John lose his footing and sent him tumbling down the mountain, hitting his head along the way and coming to rest on the narrow ledge. "Hey, are you OK?" Greg screamed out to his friend. But there was no response. "When he didn't answer I got pretty scared," says Greg. "I knew he was probably hurt bad, so I tried to get to him."

Greg tried to get as close to John as he could without endangering himself. He saw his friend frozen and terrified, clinging to the rock for dear life. His head was bleeding, and his leg was as swollen as a grapefruit from the rattler bite. Though still conscious, he looked like he was about to pass out. Greg, whose mom was a nurse and whose dad was a fireman, knew enough about emergencies to realize this was serious. "Hang on!" Greg screamed to his friend. "I'm coming!"

But Greg didn't know how he would make the final few feet over to John. There was no safe way there. What's more, he knew his friend couldn't hang on much longer. Remembers Greg, "I could see his face from where I was, and he didn't look good. He looked really scared and was crying. He looked like he was slipping off the ledge, too."

As Greg tried to come up with a solution to save his friend, John began to hallucinate from the bite. "Am I gonna die?" John cried out to his friend. But Greg immediately called back to calm him, "No, you idiot, you are not going to die. You're my best friend. You can't die. I'm going to get you out of here." Greg had to think quick. There was no time to run the two miles back home and get help, and no way to call for anyone. It was up to Greg to save his best friend. "I knew I couldn't let him give up," says Greg. "I had to make him fight because if he slipped again then he would die."

An expert climber, Greg soon realized there was no way he could safely make it over to his friend and get them both back to safety. John would have to either slide over to him or drop into Greg's arms if Greg could maneuver himself over to a safe spot a few feet below the ledge where John was. Considering John's present condition he knew the latter was the only option.

But most importantly, he knew he had to keep John from passing out because he remembered his mother telling him how people frequently fell unconscious after head injuries. So quick-thinking Greg started asking John to name all the Nintendo games he had. "My mom always told me that if somebody hits their head, you have to keep them awake," explains Greg. "He has hundreds of those games, so I knew it would keep him from falling asleep if he was talking about them."

As soon as Greg made it to a safe spot below his friend, he instructed John to reach up and unsnag his backpack from the branch; he then told John to slide down the ledge and he would catch him below. But John was fading fast and was terrified to move. "I can't do it," John cried. "It won't work. I'm gonna die!"

Greg knew he had to keep his friend going, so he challenged him. "You told me you were a better climber than me!" Greg screamed at John. "Prove it!" But John was quickly losing consciousness. Greg had to think of something else to inspire his friend. He suddenly re-membered a recent incident when John was confronted by a school bully. "Hey, remember when stupid Scotty called you a wimp and you beat him at basketball even after you were six baskets down?" But John was still not responding. "Hey, you're my best friend and you have to get down with me or I'm gonna get in a lotta trouble!" Greg cried.

Incredibly, it was the thought of getting his friend in trouble that inspired John to push harder than he thought he could. He opened his eyes, reached up and unsnagged the backpack, and then he looked down at Greg. "I promise I won't let you get in trouble," said John. He then closed his eyes and slowly slid down, still clinging to the bottom of the ledge with his hands.

But he would have to let go completely to slide the next five feet down to his friend. "Let go!" yelled Greg. "I'm here, I promise I'll catch you!" John let go, and his mangled body fell like a sack of potatoes into Greg's arms. "Got you!" Greg screamed as he caught John's backpack strap and then grabbed John. Greg ripped off his shirt and made a tourniquet to wrap around John's head to stop the bleeding. Then he took John's shirt and ripped it up to wrap around his leg where the snake had struck.

The boys quickly made it down the rest of the mountain with John's arms around Greg's neck. Then John passed out cold. "I got really scared at first that he was dead," remembers Greg. "But my mom taught me how to check for a pulse, and he was still alive. I tried to wake him but I couldn't." Amazingly, Greg decided to carry his friend the two miles home for help. "I couldn't just leave him there," says Greg. "I didn't know if I'd make it back in time to save him." He slumped his pal over his back and hiked the two miles in a record half hour.

His mom, the nurse, rushed them all to the hospital.

Just minutes later John was in the emergency room. He had suffered a concussion, lost lots of blood and needed immediate anti-venom treatment, but less than a few hours later he was out of danger and asking for his friend Greg.

"I walked into the room and he looks up and smiles and says, 'You're my hero!' " remembers Greg. "I didn't feel like a hero because I knew he would have done the same for me. We're best friends for life."

Straight A's in Love

Chuck was the class clown, and he loved making everybody laugh.

But Chuck had a hard life from the very beginning. His father died when he was six and his mother was in and out of hospitals with lung cancer from the time he was ten. Left by himself most of the time with no one around to care for him, the confused youth soon began relying on drugs to numb his pain and loneliness. He quickly became an addict and dropped out of school. Selling drugs on the streets of Little Rock, Arkansas, in the early 1980s became the only way sixteen-year-old Chuck could feed his own drug habit. By the time he was seventeen, he was so hooked on crack cocaine and heroin, he could barely make it an hour without a fix.

Ironically, the high-school dropout's best hope for the future came from three straight-A students—Phil, Van and Barbara. "We all thought he was funny," says Barbara. "And he was nice to us. We were always getting picked on at school, and he was the only one who used to help us or stand up for us. He wasn't really our best friend or anything, but we felt kind of grateful to him for sticking up for us."

After Chuck dropped out of high school, he started hanging out on the streets around the school where the three honor students would see him every day. "He would always be there in the morning to talk to some of his old friends," says Phil. "Sometimes he'd try and play basketball with the guys at lunch, but they usually just made fun of him and told him to get lost."

One day while trying to pick a community service project for their senior civics class, they came up with an idea to help Chuck. Each student was required to complete a set number of hours of volunteer work during their final year at school, so the three geniuses decided to use the assignment to help their wayward pal. They would unofficially adopt Chuck, each taking care of him for a day or two a week by being his friend and hanging out with him—maybe even taking him home for dinner and letting him spend the night at one of their houses—in an effort to get him off the streets and off drugs. "At first it was just a crazy idea to make our service requirement easier," admits Van, "but then we got serious about it."

The freewheeling whiz kids pitched the idea to their parents, teachers and then to Chuck. "We really believed that if we just gave him a little love and compassion we could clean him up," says Barbara. "Our teacher approved the project, but she warned us that it might be too much for us to handle. I don't think we even began to understand what she meant."

With nowhere else to go and willing to do anything to get out of his mom's house, he agreed to hang out with them a few days a week. But the eager altruists soon found that helping an addict was harder than they thought. "We didn't really understand anything about drug abuse," says Barbara. "We thought it would be easy to clean him up."

Problems with their new project first began when Chuck began showing up high at their houses in front of their parents. But the young guardian angel wannabes wouldn't give up; in fact, they were more determined than ever. "We might have started out as a way to get out of an assignment or just to see if we could do it," says Barbara. "But now we were really concerned about him. Deep down he was a sweet and caring guy, but he was in trouble and needed our help."

However, just as their devotion to their cause deepened, an unexpected obstacle arose when the school, fearing Chuck's criminal involvement would endanger the youths, warned them they might be expelled if they continued their association with Chuck. "It was unbelievable," says Phil. "We were trying to help Chuck get off drugs and teach him how to take care of himself, which is what school is supposed to be about, and they were threatening to punish us. I really lost respect for our principal at that point."

But they weren't going to give up on Chuck. The stellar students took a vote and decided if they got kicked out, they would just go straight into college. But nothing would deter them from helping Chuck. Their parents agreed to let them continue helping him if they could convince him to check into a drug rehab center and go straight.

With Chuck's mom's permission, the three of them and their parents arranged to pick him up and bring him in together. At first he agreed, but when it came time to go, he was nowhere to be found. "We looked everywhere," says Barbara. "I started crying because I thought maybe he did something stupid. He was so down about everything, and he was really starting to think bad thoughts. I remember him telling me a few days earlier how easy it was to kill yourself by overdosing on heroin because it just felt like falling asleep."

Meanwhile, Chuck was confused and wasting away in a crack house a mile from his home. "My head was so messed up from the drugs I didn't care about anything," recalls Chuck. "Plus the image I had of myself was so low, I didn't think I could ever do what they wanted me to. I just couldn't imagine a life without drugs. I really liked them, but I didn't believe I could ever have my act together like they did."

But his newfound friends would not desert him. For the next two days they took shifts waiting at his house and searched the streets until he finally came home looking half dead. Then they flew into action. "We kidnapped him," says Van. "We just grabbed him, no questions asked. He was pretty wasted from all the drugs, so it wasn't really that tough." They handcuffed their unwilling patient and threw him in Barbara's car. She drove while the others held him. Though visibly upset, he never raised a finger to his caring captors.

As they entered the rehab center, Chuck broke down and cried. "It was so sad," remembers Barbara. "I never ever saw anything like that before. He was really scared. And that's when I realized that he was just this little kid inside that was hurting and wanted to feel better but didn't know where to run to for help."

Chuck stayed at the center for the next six weeks and emerged a completely different person. He'd kicked his drug habit and was ready to go back to school. "I didn't even recognize him," says Barbara. "He was pretty cute all cleaned up." The three Good Samaritans immediately embraced their friend and told him how much they loved him.

That night at a local video arcade where they went to celebrate, they all promised to love and support each other for the rest of their lives. "All I knew at that point was that I really was indebted to them," remembers Chuck. "Their friendship and support saved my life and I was going to try my best to be worthy of what they did."

The very next year Chuck went back to school and graduated. Then he was accepted into state college and while his three friends all went to other universities, they would never forget the bond they shared or the promise they made. "We never lost touch with each other," says Barbara. "None of us would let that happen."

Chuck earned his finance degree and went on to work for a major international management firm. Meanwhile, Phil and Van became computer programmers and Barbara became an English literature professor. A decade after their lifesaving mission gave Chuck back his future, he was able to come to his friends' rescue.

Hurting for capital, Phil and Van's new Internet company was headed for bankruptcy until Chuck loaned them his life savings in order to bail them out. With Chuck's money and advice, Phil and Van's company quickly achieved tremendous success, and they were able to sell it less than two years later for five times what they had put into it, enabling them to pay back Chuck with substantial interest. "He always used to tell us we saved his life," says Phil. "Well, he saved our skin when he gave us that money."

Nowadays, though they all live in different parts of the country, Van, Barbara, Phil and Chuck are still as close as can be. "I think Barbara puts it best," says Chuck. "She says we are all so close you'd think we were connected at the heart. It sounds goofy, but it's true."

A Mother's Touch

~~

The summer of 1986 was a good one for Ruby. The twenty-six-year-old Maryland woman had just gotten a great job as a bookkeeper for a major Baltimore construction firm and she was finally starting to make her dreams of independence come true. She had paid back her student loans, and now could afford to move out of her mom's house and get a place of her own. She was healthy, well-employed, had plenty of friends and not a care in the world. "I was having the time of my life," remembers Ruby. "Everything was perfect. I was dating a couple of different guys and just having fun. I was finally on my own."

When one of those guys asked Ruby to join him and

some friends for a day of Jet Ski fun, she was ready and willing. "I was a little scared because I'd never been on one before," admits Ruby, "but I figured what could happen? I always thought Jet Skis were pretty safe."

The day started harmlessly enough. Her friend arrived at her apartment bright and early at 10 A.M. on a hot Saturday in July. It was already pushing 85 degrees by mid-morning. She said good-bye to her cat, Hazel, grabbed her bathing suit and sunscreen and headed out.

As they neared the beach, she became a little nervous about her lack of Jet Ski experience but figured she'd be fine. At a dock a few miles from the beach they met up with their friends, who were loading the Jet Skis into the water. By the time they arrived Ruby was ready to go. "Hop on, Ruby," her friend told her. Hiding her trepidation, she took off her shirt, rubbed some sunscreen on herself and got on. Feeling the hum of the mighty machine below her, she waited for her friends to load the other Jet Skis into the water. Then they all were off.

Ruby fumbled to work the controls, while trying to keep up with her friend. But then as they cleared the channel and headed into the ocean, Ruby over-accelerated just as a huge wave came her way. Ruby and the Jet Ski flipped upside down, and then the mighty machine came crashing down on the base of her spine. As she plunged beneath the waves, her friends and life-guards rushed to her rescue, then hurried her to a nearby hospital.

When she awoke, her mother, Ali, and a doctor were standing over her, her mom holding her hand as tight as she could. "The first words I heard were from my mother," says Ruby. " 'I want you to remember you are going to be as good as new,' she told me." When Ruby asked what had happened, the doctor responded, "You took a massive blow to the spine from the full weight of a Jet Ski, and you are lucky to be alive."

As Ruby tried hopelessly to lift her head up to see her mother and the doctor better, she quickly realized she could not move at all, and she was suddenly petrified. "What's wrong?" she screamed out to her mother. "Why can't I move?" While she shrieked in terror, the doctor and her mother tried in vain to calm her. Her mother insisted the doctor leave for a moment. Then she started to comfort her daughter. "I'll let the doctor explain all the details," said her mother. "But basically it's going to take some time to get back on your feet. But I want you to promise me that whatever the doctor tells you, you won't give up. Promise me!"

Still drowsy from the accident, Ruby struggled to understand just exactly what her mother was trying to say, but she was baffled. All she knew was that she could not move and even breathing was a struggle. "I want to see the doctor!" she screamed at her mother. "I want to see him now!"

After what seemed like an eternity to Ruby the doctor

appeared with her mother leading the way. "What is wrong with me?" she asked, hoping not to hear what she already knew. Then came that horrible word—paralyzed! She had suffered severe damage to her spinal cord, and she might never regain any feeling or mobility below her waist. She would never walk again. "I felt like my life was over," remembers Ruby. "I had just gained my independence, and it was all gone just like that. I was an invalid."

But her mother wouldn't leave it at that. "Can you swear to me that my daughter will not walk again?" she asked the doctor. When the startled doctor did not answer, her mother shot back, "You listen to me, Ruby, you will walk again. In fact, you are going to run. I guarantee it."

Overwhelmed by the tragedy, Ruby fell into a deep depression over the next month. When the day came for her to leave the hospital in a wheelchair, it took all of Ruby's strength just to wake up that morning. "I really didn't care about anything," says Ruby. "Looking back, I know it sounds like I was being awfully selfish. After all, there are so many physically challenged people who lead very meaningful and fulfilling lives, but I just wanted to die." But fortunately Ruby's mom had enough courage and determination for both of them. "I love my daughter like nobody else in this world," says her mom. "And if there was a chance that she could one day walk again, I was determined to make that happen."

Ali took her daughter home to her house where she had already had a spare room converted into a gym with just about every piece of athletic rehabilitation equipment she could find. She refused to listen to the doctor's advice that she give her daughter a few days after she left the hospital to adjust to her handicap before beginning therapy. "I told the doctor my daughter wouldn't be in that chair longer than six months, and there was no time to waste. It wasn't that I couldn't love her in her condition. But I wasn't going to let her give up on recovering until we tried everything. I loved her too much to let her down that way."

Ali spent countless hours investigating every single high-energy, high-protein diet to get Ruby in the best possible shape. She studied everything she could get her hands on regarding muscle and nerve regeneration and healing, day and night. And every day she woke her daughter up at 6 A.M. to start her regimen of physical activity. "I felt like I was in boot camp," reveals Ruby. "I hated her for doing this to me. But by the third or fourth week, I really started to believe that I would walk again. I mean, she just insisted that I would. There was absolutely no doubt in her mind. She just kept telling me how much she loved me and that all I needed to do was keep my promise to fight and believe in her, and so I did."

While Ruby worked on getting her upper body in the

best shape it had ever been, her mother spent hours every day working her legs in countless stretching exercises. Hourly massages and pep talks kept Ruby's mother busy from sunup to sundown. She cooked meals every day for her daughter to make sure she had the best food and best nutrition. "I don't know how to explain it but about six months after this routine began I swear I could feel my mother's hands touching my legs during one of the rubdowns."

Then one day with no warning, her mother confidently told Ruby that it was time to stand up. "I thought she was crazy," remembers Ruby. "But every time I looked at her, her eyes were so full of love and support and belief in me. It was as if I had her legs and I could walk on her strength alone." With a pair of crutches for Ruby to brace herself, slowly her mother picked her up out of her wheelchair. Ruby's now-muscular arms struggled to support her body with the crutches. Then slowly and nervously she tried to shift her weight to her legs, but she quickly fell back into the wheelchair. Her mother smiled and gave Ruby the thumbs-up sign.

For the next year, every single day started with Ruby's mother bringing a set of crutches into the room and laboring through the impossible process of getting her up on them. And every day Ruby would fall. But her mother never gave up any hope and Ruby kept trying to walk. "Every morning, we had so much fun," recalls

Ruby. "I really started to forget I couldn't walk after awhile. She made me feel as if I just had a sprained ankle or something."

Ruby's mom also made sure her daughter kept her spirits up and encouraged Ruby to have friends over and even go out on dates. She had Ruby looking for jobs that she could start when she could walk again. She rented inspirational movies for her to watch. And only once did her mother even acknowledge the possibility of her being unable to walk again.

"One day I got a little depressed," remembers Ruby. "I asked her what if I didn't get better, then what? And she looked at me very sweetly and said, 'If you turned into a frog tomorrow, I would still love you and support you just as much.'"

Ali continued her relentless support of her daughter every day and every hour, never weakening under the strain, only getting stronger, and every day Ruby swore she could feel a little more.

Meanwhile, the doctors still insisted the feelings were phantom memories. But Ali was certain her daughter was on the road to recovery. "I knew all Ruby needed was love," says Ali. "I really don't know how I knew. I just did."

Then it happened. Only a year and a half after the accident, which doctors said would leave her in a wheel-chair for the rest of her life, Ruby felt her toes tingle one day and then wiggled them the next. "At first I just thought I was imagining things," says Ruby. "But my mother was right there in the room with me when it happened, and she just looked at me with a great big smile on her face and said, 'See, I told you.' " Over the next three or four months Ruby and her mother defied doctors almost on a daily basis as she slowly but surely progressed from moving her toes to her feet and eventually her legs. Within five months' time, she was walking on crutches. "I never doubted for one moment that I would see my daughter walk again," says her mom. "And I knew the important thing to do was to keep her convinced of that."

Till this day doctors are still unable to explain Ruby's recovery. "The odds of her ever walking again were actually much lower than I ever told her," says one of her doctors. "One in ten million people has the type of recovery she did. I can only say that there are things about nerve and muscle regeneration that we still don't understand, things that Ruby's mom was able to capitalize on. Love is a very strong component of any type of healing."

And no one knows that better than Ruby, who now works as a physical trainer helping others like herself regain the physical skills they've lost after injuries. "I always knew my mom loved me, but I never realized until this happened just how much that love mattered," says Ruby. "If I can give that kind of help and love to somebody else, maybe I can make a few more miracles happen—wouldn't that be nice?"

You Can't Steal Love

~

*C*arlos committed his first crime when he was just ten years old. He and some friends took the money out of the cash register where one of them had a job as a stock boy in an El Paso, Texas, drugstore. "It was easy and I thought it was kind of fun at the time," remembers Carlos. "All my friends were doing it, and I knew it was wrong, but I didn't want to be left out."

From then on he began stealing anything he could and hung out on the streets of El Paso. An older friend then taught him how to break into cars when he was thirteen, and he began heisting radios and turning them over at a local pawnshop for $10 each. He moved up to stealing whole cars by the time he was sixteen, making

$500 for each from a local chop shop across the border in Mexico. Then he started selling drugs for a local ganglord who was connected to a Colombian drug cartel. "That was definitely where the big money was," reveals Carlos. "And I went straight to the top working for them."

While making a killing selling narcotics, he and his pals started holding up convenience stores just for thrills. And no matter how much his mother, Rosalie, tried to teach him or discipline him, she couldn't break through his hardening heart. "I was buying nice clothes and I always had money in my pockets," remembers Carlos. "I thought that was the American way. That was success to me. My mom tried to teach me it was wrong. But there was no way she could compete with the money and the excitement. I was addicted to it."

His role models were gangbangers and the bad guys from Hollywood movies like *Scarface*'s Tony Montana. He figured he'd hit it big and then retire rich. But before he knew it, he was standing before a judge being sentenced to three years in prison for holding up a convenience store when he was eighteen. "I was proud of getting caught," admits Carlos. "I thought of going to prison like it was training—it would give me the chance to learn from guys on the inside how to be."

And Carlos was right. Behind bars he met the right kind of people to further his career. He learned tricks of the trade and met his next partners in crime. "If I felt I was wrong," explains Carlos, "then prison might have reformed me, but I believed my only mistake was getting caught, so I tried learning how not to get caught. That was my goal."

Carlos was paroled after a year and a half and immediately resumed his life of crime. Incredibly, he even refused to let his mother pick him up the day he was released, opting instead to make a delivery of drugs for a gang boss on the way home to visit his family. It was a simple job, but when the buy turned out to be a police sting operation, Carlos found himself back in jail less than twenty-four hours after getting out, this time nabbed for selling drugs and violating his parole with possession of a firearm. His mother was devastated when he called her from the cell with the shocking news of his arrest only hours after he had been released. "She had this big party for me with all my cousins and my grandma there," explains Carlos. "When I never showed up, they got so worried. She called all the hospitals to see where I was. When I called and told her what happened, she just wouldn't stop crying. That was bad, real bad. But I remember she said she loved me before she hung up even though she was so upset. I always remembered that."

This time Carlos would be sentenced to five years in prison. And even his sister gave up on him. "He was no good," says his sister, Sylvia. "And I didn't want him breaking my mother's heart any more." But his mother still refused to give up on him. She visited him almost every day in prison, bringing him cookies and handwritten reminders of how much he was loved and didn't need crime to make him important. "She'd give me these letters about forgiveness and how it was never too late in God's eyes or hers to be a good man," Carlos fondly remembers. "And she was never really mad at me. She would just cry and that was worse. I couldn't take that because I really loved her down deep. But I thought I knew everything."

Carlos continued to idolize and learn from the gang leaders behind bars, until finally he felt like they were his new family. "I had to hang with those guys to get through, but I liked them too," admits Carlos. "I felt like I was one of them, and I thought those were the people I belonged with."

But meanwhile his real family was doing all they could to help him. His mother was petitioning the parole board every year for his early release. "She would come down every time I was up for parole and bring pictures of me in church when I was a little boy and beg them to let me out." But Carlos was a constant problem in prison. His fights, his mixing with gangs and his many offenses behind bars this time would ensure that he served every day of his five-year sentence.

By the time he got out of prison, he was twenty-five, and his loving mom was there to greet him. But again the career criminal-in-the-making wouldn't even let her take him home. Instead, he accepted a ride arranged for him by a gang lord he was planning to work for. "I knew I was breaking my mother's heart," says Carlos. "But I was so out of it, I didn't care. I couldn't feel anything." Even as he left his devoted mom standing there in the midday sun, she sent him off with a kiss and an invitation to change his life and come home anytime.

Over the next two years, Carlos became a major player in the Texas drug trade, smuggling drugs back and forth across the border and in from South America. He had learned well in prison, and was now an expert at avoiding detection or capture. He was soon a wanted man by the U.S. Drug Enforcement Agency and his various names and photos were plastered all over Texas and the southwestern United States. His bosses decided he was better used outside of the country handling shipments and production—a definite promotion in rank and responsibility. But he could no longer come back into this country. He sent a letter to his family explaining to them that he would not see them again. His mother was once again brokenhearted. "I told her to forget about him," remembers his sister. "But he was so important to her and she never stopped loving him."

Despite Carlos's farewell, at least three or four times

a year his mother risked her life to search out the local drug lords and deliver birthday cards and messages for her son wherever he was. Some actually made it to him. "She could have wound up dead just talking to these people," marvels Carlos. "Whenever I would get one of those cards it would kill me inside. I wanted her to forget about me, but she wouldn't give up. She'd always write, 'I will never desert my son, I love him forever.'"

For three years she kept up hope while Carlos ran drug operations outside the country. And the cards kept coming. Carlos would tell himself that he no longer had a family. The drugs and the money were his family now. But secretly he looked forward to those cards. However, on his thirtieth birthday no card came.

Carlos was shocked when he found out through his sources the awful truth—his mother was dying. A massive stroke had left her totally paralyzed and barely alive. The thought of actually losing his mother forever shocked Carlos. He suddenly felt a rush of guilt about his life and the pain he had brought to his mother. "I felt that it was all my fault," reveals Carlos. "I thought that if I hadn't of done what I did and treated her so bad, it wouldn't have happened. I didn't want her to die. I realized all of a sudden how much I loved her." Worst of all, Carlos knew there was no way he could see his mother. If he stepped back into the United States, he risked being caught or killed. Not to mention that his bosses had prohibited him from ever returning.

That's when his mother came to him in a vision while he slept. "She was begging me to change my life before she died, telling me it wasn't too late," says Carlos of the incredible dream. " 'Go to the police, they will protect you,' she kept saying to me. I knew it was a vision. I knew more than ever how much I loved my mother. I had to see her." Carlos decided he'd sneak across the border at night knowing full well that his mother's house could be under surveillance at any time. If word leaked out that he was back, he would be immediately arrested or worse, killed by his own people, figuring that he would get caught and cut a deal to save his own skin.

Carlos made it over the border and to his mother's house under the cover of darkness. He arrived at the house in the wee hours of the morning and sneaked in through an open window. He found his mother in her bed. His sister, sleeping by her side, woke up when she heard Carlos creep in. "I would have turned him in the second I saw him," says Sylvia. "But my mother was so sick. And I knew all she wanted was to see him." When Carlos saw how sick his mother was, he fell to his knees and cried at her bedside. "I saw her there and she looked so old," says Carlos. "I saw the pain that I caused her, and I prayed for her and begged her to forgive me. But she was just lying there."

As his sister began yelling at him, suddenly his mother turned her head for the first time since she had been out of the hospital and spoke. "She said, 'I still love you Carlos, you are my little one,' in Spanish." His mother's simple words melted Carlos's heart instantly and left him begging for her forgiveness. But what followed was nothing short of a miracle. "Everything seemed to be clear to me all of a sudden," explains Carlos. "I knew I had to turn myself in and try to turn my life around. I never killed anyone or anything like that, so I knew I still could change. That's the first time I ever thought anything like that." Before he knew it he was saying words he never thought he'd hear coming from his mouth. "I told her, 'I love you, Mom, and I'm going straight right now.'" remembers Carlos. "Then I picked up the phone and called the police." A big smile came across his mother's face. And his sister was awestruck. "I really thought he was too far gone until he made that call," remembers Sylvia. "We just started crying together."

Carlos agreed to help law enforcement officials prosecute drug lords in exchange for witness protection and a small sentence secured in solitary confinement. His mother lived for two more years, long enough to see her son free and straight for the first time in almost twenty years. "They arranged for me to see her when I got out of jail right before I went into the protection program," says Carlos. "She was weak, but I could tell she was happy. It was like I was the only thing that had gone wrong in her life, and I fixed that. If it wasn't for her never giving up on me I know I would be dead today," insists Carlos. "I can still feel her inside me, and I'll always love her, like she always loved me."

A Gamble Worth Taking

Cecilia loved her sister, Kate, so much that there wasn't anything she wouldn't do for her. After the two girls' mother died of cancer when they were teenagers, their father abandoned them, leaving Cecilia the important but difficult job of looking out for her younger, adventurous sister. This wasn't easy because all Kate wanted to do was cash in on the good life of drinking and partying. Cecilia worked two jobs her senior year in high school to make sure she and Kate could afford their apartment and to put food on the table. And she made sure her sister stayed in school and graduated.

Las Vegas in 1967, where Kate and Cecilia lived, was a town filled with more organized crime leaders than

New York. While millions of money-hungry gamblers were living it up on the Strip and dreaming of being rich, the underworld was making millions of dollars under the table. For those that lived and worked in the money-making mecca, it was a place where hopefully fantasies could one day come true for them too.

One of those fantasies belonged to Kate, who was a cocktail waitress at one of the city's most famous casinos. She was only nineteen when she met smooth-talking Ricky while serving him drinks. He routinely wagered thousands of dollars at the casino without a thought of whether he won or lost. Kate had noticed the tall, dark and charming young man many times before. She was attracted to his sharp silk suits, his slick, clean-cut look and his cocky smile. Often working two shifts to make ends meet, Kate was impressed by his big tips and kind words. "She was young and looking for Mr. Right to sweep her off her feet," remembers her sister, Cecilia. "And she thought why not find a rich Mr. Right instead of a poor one? She was a little hell-raiser and she just wanted to have fun. I think she knew I'd always help her, so she liked living life on the edge."

Cecilia worked as a clerk for the city court, where every day she saw the criminal activity that was an unavoidable part of the Vegas gambling fortune. The minute Cecilia heard of slick Ricky, she didn't trust him. "It was so easy to see that he was doing something illegal," says Cecilia. "He didn't have a real job to speak of. He wore suits that cost a fortune, and he was always in the casino being real buddy-buddy with the bad boys who ran it. But Kate thought he was her way out of working ever again, and she didn't want to believe he was a criminal."

One day after her shift, Ricky asked Kate out to dinner. He swept her off her feet and whisked her away to Los Angeles for the weekend. For the next three months he wined and dined her, flew her to New York and Chicago for whirlwind weekends and bought her expensive clothes and jewelry. "He told her he was a freelance jeweler," recalls Cecilia. "And she believed him because she wanted to be in love. She wanted somebody to love her so bad, but she didn't just want a guy from around town. She wanted the brass ring."

As Kate and Ricky became more serious with each other, Cecilia grew increasingly worried about her beloved Kate. "All of a sudden the two of them are making all these plans together!" remembers Cecilia. "That's when I started warning her. 'If you think you are gonna marry this guy or anything like that you are crazy,' I told her. 'This guy's a crook. He's going to get you in trouble!'"

But the final straw for Cecilia came one night when Ricky made a play for her behind Kate's back. "Here's this guy who already knows I don't like him dating my baby sister, and he's trying to put the moves on me," says Cecilia. "He was disgusting, and when he did that I decided I had to do something." But Kate refused to hear anything negative about her beau. After Cecilia stopped giving her sister messages from Ricky when he called the house, Kate terrified her sister by telling her she and Ricky were planning to move in together, and that she would never speak to Cecilia again. "I knew she was serious," says Cecilia. "I knew exactly what the deal was. He was going to put her up in some fancy apartment and keep her there while he went out and did whatever he wanted to do with God knows who. I knew he was a crook and dangerous but I just didn't know how to prove it to her. But I had to do something. I loved her. She was my baby sister."

Cecilia's position at the courthouse allowed her to access personal information on Vegas residents, so she immediately ran Ricky's name through the files. Except for a few speeding tickets and unpaid parking tickets, nothing showed up. She knew she had to take more drastic measures to help her sister. So she told Kate to arrange for the three of them to go out to dinner pretending she wanted to patch things up with her sister and Ricky. "I thought the only way I was going to find out about this guy was if I got friendly with him. I had to convince him that I liked him, so I turned on the charm."

Dressed in her sexiest dress, Cecilia met her sister and

Ricky at a local posh restaurant that night where they ate and drank till dawn. When her sister wasn't looking she slipped Ricky a note that asked him to call her when Kate was at work. The next day she received a phone call from Ricky and the two agreed to meet for a date at his place. "I was burning up the whole time I was talking to him on the phone," reveals Cecilia. "But I played it like I was really into him and that my sister was a little punk and all that. He bought it all, and he talked about her like she was nothing. I wanted to kill him, but I had to stick to my plan."

A few days later, they met at Ricky's apartment and immediately he brought her into the bedroom. She slyly convinced him to get undressed and then to wait in the bathroom while she got ready. She would tell him when to come out. And just as she had hoped, Ricky left his wallet and address book on the dresser. She rifled through them, copying down as many names, numbers and details as she could that might be able to give her a lead on his real story. She hid the information in one of her shoes. Then she called to Ricky to come back out and told him she had to use the bathroom herself. After hiding out for almost a half hour faking an upset stomach, she informed him she was sick and had to leave.

The next day she gave all the information to a trusted friend at the police department and three days later she received a full report back on the mysterious "Mr.

Right." "Everyone he knew or had contact with was a criminal or involved with criminals," says Cecilia. "I knew he was no good. Now I had proof."

But Cecilia realized it wasn't going to be enough to convince Kate. Determined to save the sister she loved, she decided she would need to infiltrate the deadly Las Vegas underworld in order to get the goods on Ricky. While putting Ricky off by telling him she was working overtime for a few weeks, she spent the next month embedding herself in the seedy underbelly of Las Vegas. Donning her most revealing outfits, she hung out at the Strip's hottest casinos, meeting the city's high rollers and casino kingpins. Using a fake name and pretending she was an aspiring showgirl who was willing to do whatever it took to get a break, she was quickly able to win the affections and the confidence of some of the town's biggest crime bosses.

Within a few short weeks, she was living the very life she was trying to protect her sister from, drinking and partying all night with drug lords and mobsters and even sleeping with many of them. "I'll tell you now I had to do some things that I'm not proud of," Cecilia recalls tearfully. "But when I found out what kind of trouble my sister was getting into, there was really no price that was too high to save her. I wasn't going to let anything happen to her." The whole time Cecilia was leading her double life, she knew that if Ricky ever appeared in the same room as her at the same time, her cover would be blown, and it would probably cost her life. "I really didn't care," reveals Cecilia. "I had already lost my parents, and I'd rather die than stand by and let anything happen to my little sister. She was worth the risk."

Then, in an intimate moment with one of the mobsters, she discovered the terrifying truth about Ricky while secretly tape-recording the conversation. "I asked what he did," explains Cecilia. "I figured he would say Ricky was a bookie or something like that. So I didn't know what this guy was so startled for when I mentioned Ricky's name." The stunned mobster asked her how she knew of Ricky and when she said it was from the casino, he warned her to stay away from the desperate man. "This guy, who was no angel himself, turned all white and said, 'If you want to live, I would stay clear of that guy.' "

After pressing the point, Cecilia discovered her sister's lover was a hired killer! "I just got cold all over when I heard that," remembers Cecilia. "I couldn't show that I cared, but when I got home that night, I was as sick as a dog. She was about to move in with an assassin!" Later that night she told her sister the whole story and played her the incriminating tape. Kate was dumbfounded and scared. "For the first time ever she didn't answer me back," says Cecilia. "She was terrified, but at least she finally believed me."

Kate begged Cecilia to help her break up with Ricky, and she promised to listen to whatever her big sister told her to do. But Cecilia was sure Ricky would never let her sister go, so she quickly arranged for Kate to go stay with a friend in San Francisco one weekend when Ricky was out of town. When Ricky returned, Kate called him and told him she had to go to Seattle to visit a sick friend.

While Kate used the lie to hold him off, Cecilia quickly packed up a few last prized possessions and left town, later meeting her sister in San Francisco. "I was scared to death that I was going to be killed until the moment I got on that plane!" reveals Cecilia. "I never admitted it to Kate at the time, but the only thing that kept me together was that I knew I had to protect her."

Kate and Cecilia never returned to Las Vegas and were never again bothered by Ricky or any other mobsters. Kate finally met a nice man and settled down to have a daughter and lead a good and happy life, while Cecilia married and had two sons herself. The sisters are now both living somewhere in the northeastern United States.

Kate has no doubt she owes her life and her happiness to the sister who risked everything for the one she loved. And ever since that unforgettable night when Cecilia told her the truth about Ricky, she has done her best to look out for her big sister with the same devotion. "She gave up so much for me and she could have been killed," proclaims Kate. "I doubt I can ever repay her for all that she did, but I will love her with all my heart till the day I die. And I would lay down my life for her if she ever needed me to."

Speaking of Love . . .

~∽

*A*fter a diving accident left Lance paralyzed from the neck down, doctors told him that besides being robbed of his movement, he would never speak again. The accident had traumatized speech centers in his brain as well as paralyzing his vocal cords, making it impossible for him to talk.

Lance had already won two world championship riding rings by the time he was twenty-three. But when the six-foot-four cowboy dove into a river outside Ft. Worth, Texas, and hit a hidden tree trunk that broke his neck, his riding days were over. Lance was in a coma and doctors doubted he would even survive the night.

But his father never even let that possibility enter his

mind. "I knew he would make it," remembers his dad, P. D. "And I refused to leave his side. I made them bring in a wheelchair for me so I could sleep in the room with him."

The next day while P. D. hovered over his son, he received his first miracle as Lance awoke from his coma after thirty-six hours. But his son spent the next seven months in intensive care with pneumonia and a series of breathing problems. And all the time he couldn't speak a word to his dad or the rest of his family to let them know what he was thinking or how he was feeling. He was trapped in a world of silence. But that didn't stop P. D. from finding a way to break that sound barrier with the son he loved. "I started working out signals with him so we could understand each other," explains P. D. "I wasn't going to let him feel like he was alone. I stayed with him every step of the way and we found a way to talk."

One day while Lance lay upside down strapped to his gurney in the hospital, his father got on the floor and crawled underneath his son so he could look into his eyes. Then he made him a promise he would keep forever. "I told him as long as I was alive, no matter how tough it was or what he needed, I would never put him in a nursing home or a care facility," remembers P. D. "I would take care of him myself. I could see the smile come to his face when I said that."

After Lance emerged from intensive care he was allowed to go home, but his father understood from now on he and the rest of his family would all need to devote themselves to taking care of Lance and giving him all the love he needed. An electrical contractor, P. D. immediately set out to help his son however he could, inventing and teaching Lance to use hundreds of devices that would make life easier for him. "He was my son, and I had to help him whatever his situation was," says P. D. "Since I was good with electronics, that was an easy way for me to use what I knew to assist him."

Over the next year, he taught Lance to communicate by gripping a pointer stick between his teeth and spelling out words on a wooden alphabet board. He adapted a special keyboard on one of the first generations of computers to allow his son to tap out words using a mouthpiece that acted as his hands. And they learned to use the computer together to give his son a way to communicate with the world and feel as strong and capable as everyone else. P. D. developed signals for hundreds of words, so he and his son could have their own special language. He and his wife, as well as their other two sons, took on the awesome task of caring for Lance, who literally could do nothing for himself. From dressing to eating or bathing and using the bathroom, he was essentially an invalid. They had to refit the whole house with special doors, bathrooms, ramps and anything else that would allow their son the freedom he needed.

But what they were only beginning to learn was that what Lance couldn't do with his body, he made up for with his heart. "Sometimes I would be tired or worn out from work," says P. D., "and he would look at me with a big smile and tell me in our special signs how much he loved me and how great I was. And then he'd tell me a joke or do something aimed at making me laugh. Here he was in his condition reminding me how blessed we all were and trying to make me feel good. That's an amazing boy."

Little by little his father worked with him to develop more words and language, trying anything he could to bring back his speech. Meanwhile, he took Lance to doctor after doctor in search of any hope for a cure. "Of course my ultimate dream and belief was that I would see him walk again," says P. D. "At the very least I wanted to be able to hear his sweet voice again. But the doctors all told me the same thing all the time—he'll never walk again and he'll never talk. But I wasn't going to ever stop having faith in my son. That's what love means."

For sixteen years, he and his wife stood by Lance, never doubting that someday and somehow their son would recover, all the time trying to make his life as meaningful and fulfilling as they could. "I had heard about somebody years ago who hadn't talked for fifteen years and just started talking again," says his mom, Caroll. "So I never gave up faith."

But most importantly, as P. D., his wife and their other two sons all did their best to help Lance keep the faith, they all renewed their own faith—in each other—and grew closer together as a family. "When we all pulled together to help him it somehow made us love each other even more," says P. D. "And even though Lance couldn't communicate as well as most people, he told us in a big way how to show our love for each other more. He would say how we all had so much to be thankful for because we had each other."

Besides his home health care, Lance was forced to undergo countless operations and hospital stays over the years to maintain his body. So when doctors ordered yet another procedure to add a type of artificial bladder to help Lance, P. D. thought nothing unusual would occur.

The relatively simple procedure was successful. Lance woke up and looked at his father, who was there as always by his son's bedside. But then, as his father stood over him smiling assuredly to let him know everything was all right, Lance shocked his father. He spoke for the first time in sixteen years, saying the words his father could only dream him uttering. "He looked at me and said, 'Pop, I love you,' " joyously recalls P. D. "I swear I started crying like a baby. I was as happy as a dad could be, and I knew that it was a miracle."

Since the surgery had nothing to do with any speech-related areas of his brain or his body, doctors were unable to explain in any way how and why he recaptured his ability to speak. "There's no medical explanation for what happened," says a hospital spokesperson. "We have to go along with the belief that it was a miracle."

Though Lance always had faith that one day he would be cured, he accepted the fate that was handed to him by living his life with dignity and grace. But it didn't take long for Lance to realize why he was granted his miracle. "Love is the most important thing in the world," says Lance. "It's all about love. God put me on this earth for some reason. Maybe it was to show people how important love is."

And Lance didn't waste any time spreading his uplifting message to the rest of the world, starting at the top with presidential hopeful and Texas governor, George W. Bush. Only a few days after his recovery, Lance told reporters he wanted to speak to the governor of his home state. "I always thought he was a very kind and compassionate leader," explains Lance. "And I thought he'd be the perfect person to share my miracle."

Within twenty-four hours Lance was on the phone with the possible future president. "Hey, Lance, how are you doing, buddy?" said Bush to his new friend. "It's great to hear your voice. I bet you feel a special feeling in your heart." And the grateful Lance wasn't shy about letting his new friend know exactly what that feeling was. Says Lance, "I asked how his family was doing, and I told him how lucky he was to have so much love."

Speaking of Love . . .

Now Lance spends hours on the Internet every day, inspiring and motivating countless new friends from every corner of the globe with his exciting story and his words of hope. But, most importantly, he can tell his family how much he truly loves them in his own words. "That's the sweetest sound I have ever heard," says P. D. "And I'll never get tired of hearing him say it."

In Love and War

At the height of World War II, sixteen-year-old Anna awoke to the cries of her family as they were torn from their small ghetto apartment in Paris. As she hid her skinny body underneath a dresser, Anna heard the bloodcurdling screams as her parents, two brothers and younger sister were beaten and dragged from their home, herself just narrowly escaping the same fate.

Hours later when she thought all was clear she scurried down the hall in search of refuge, but as luck would have it, she ran straight into the arms of Rolf, a German lieutenant who was emerging from one of the apartments. Seeing he was alone, Anna didn't run, but pretended she wasn't Jewish. A young and beautiful girl, she flirted with the officer, hoping to escape by charming him. But her girlish ways didn't fool him, and he immediately asked to see her identification papers. Realizing she was found out and fearing for her life, Anna made a break for it. But the short-legged girl didn't get very far before the lieutenant ran her down. "I was no match for his speed and strength," says Anna. "I only got a few feet or so before he caught me by the hair."

It came as no surprise to Anna that turning her in was not the first thing on his mind. "I knew he found me attractive," remembers Anna. "And he could have done anything he wanted with me, but there was a strange glint of goodness in his eyes. I somehow believed he would not hurt me." The officer asked Anna if she was hungry and when she said yes, he asked her to come home with him for supper.

"I knew it would be dangerous," reveals Anna, "but what choice did I have? So I went. I knew I was safe as long as I could keep him interested in me. The longer I could delay him turning me in, the more chances I thought I would have to escape."

Anna accompanied the officer back to the small but elegant apartment he kept in the city. He impressed the half-starved girl with a smorgasbord of food and asked her to cook for him. "He had so much of everything," recalls Anna. "There was a fresh chicken, and he had breads and jams and coffee and wine. My family had been living on soup for so long, it was more food than I had seen in years." She cooked her captor dinner and they feasted late into the night. Then, exhausted, Anna fell asleep. The next morning Anna found the soldier lying next to her with his arms around her and was surprised to learn the officer had not taken advantage of her. Reveals Anna, "I was disappointed in myself for letting my guard down with him."

When Rolf woke up, Anna thanked him for helping her. But to her surprise he looked at her and laughed, saying he didn't know what she was talking about. "That's when I became petrified again," says Anna. "I just said the first thing that came to my mind and I asked him if he needed a woman to take care of him. He was shocked." Then Rolf began to insult her. "It was as if he hated me yet liked me," explains Anna. "He hated himself for liking someone he was taught to hate and I was also angry at myself for liking him too. I know it sounds awful to say that I was so attracted to him, but I was a young girl, and he really was a handsome man. I was falling in love with him for whatever the reason."

Twenty-two-year-old Rolf had risen quickly in the German army because of his intelligence and wit. He was promoted to lieutenant because he had proved himself as a supply captain by working wonders of logistics transporting material to the troops and helping to keep the

Paris operation running smoothly. He was extremely popular in the Nazi upper ranks. Yet Anna touched something inside the young German soldier. She convinced her warden to let her stay with him, and she agreed to cook and clean for him and take care of him. He was able to falsify papers for her, which he kept under lock and key, but only under the condition she must never leave the house for any reason whatsoever. And she must be absolutely silent whenever he was gone. She obeyed.

"I was primarily a maid, but I never left the house," says Anna. "I would cook and clean, and he would come every few days or so. I know I could have run when he was away. But I felt safer there than anywhere else I could have gone."

Amazingly, despite Rolf's attraction to Anna, he was always the perfect gentleman. He was content to enjoy her well-cooked meals and company, then she'd fall asleep in his arms secure that he would never take advantage of her. "We were getting to know each other," remembers Anna. "And he was very sweet to me, bringing me home little trinkets and gifts. He didn't talk much but he listened to me and smiled no matter what I talked about. We were like a couple of kids falling in love. Soon I lost any fear that he would try and hurt me."

When the couple finally consummated their relationship for the first time three months after their extraordinary meeting, it was Anna who made the first move. The two soon were acting like husband and wife. But as Anna's fear subsided, the guilt set in. "I knew I was still hiding," says Anna. "I was just a girl, but I felt I couldn't just stand by and pretend that my people weren't dying outside those four walls. Yet I knew I couldn't leave. Where would I go? Besides, I really loved him. But I had to do something about all the others dying and being tortured."

A year to the day after they first met, Rolf came home and asked Anna to marry him. "I was shocked, happy and so confused all at the same time," says Anna. "I knew he must love me. But how could this be that we would be husband and wife when his people were killing my people?" Anna somehow summoned the strength to tell him how she felt. "If he loved me, it wouldn't matter," says Anna. "If not, I would die. I just couldn't hide anymore."

To her dismay, Rolf flew into a rage condemning her for her lack of appreciation for all that he had done for her. He informed her that because of him she was living a life that she should be grateful for. Then, after forgiving her for being Jewish, Rolf again asked her to marry him.

"I was insulted but I was fighting for my life, and I also loved him," admits Anna. "It's hard to explain. But I really did love him. And I felt I could make him see things more clearly in time, so I said yes." They married using Anna's assumed name in a town in the countryside, but still they did not tell anyone else about their relationship for the next two years.

Now it was 1943, and as the war was going badly for Germany scores of Jews were being killed while Hitler scrambled to carry out his insane "master plan" for the extermination of the Jewish race. Meanwhile, Anna was still trying to convince her husband to change his opinions and help the Jews. "I loved him like no woman ever loved her man," proclaims Anna. "I was a perfect wife. But I knew he still was uncomfortable that I was Jewish, so I couldn't talk about my feelings openly. Instead I simply spoke of right and wrong, people and love and how there were so many being hurt. I spoke of God. I even convinced him that I had turned Christian and wanted to save the other Jews so we could convert them as God wanted."

After two years, Rolf finally agreed to try and find out about her family, something she had asked him to do for years. "He told me he couldn't find them," says Anna, "but his face told me they were dead. I thought the worst for years, but when I finally found out, it was devastating for me. But he acted as if their deaths meant nothing."

Anna cried for weeks. She was beginning to believe her husband was a monster incapable of ever changing no matter how much love she gave him. But then a few days later, Rolf amazed her. "Over dinner he told me about a Jewish family found hiding in a cellar," explains Anna. "They were scheduled to be sent to a camp but instead he suggested they be used as tailors since they all knew how to sew. He pretended it was just business, but I knew getting involved with where Jews were sent was completely out of his jurisdiction, and so I knew this was his way of trying to help."

Though she knew Rolf was on the wrong side and had different beliefs than her, she felt she could make a difference in some way if she could get him to continue to use his position in whatever way he could to save lives. "I thought even if he could save just a few," remembers Anna, "then it would be something special."

Though Rolf wasn't in a decision-making position with regard to captured Jews, he was able to look the other way time and time again and influence other decision-makers to spare many lives of those destined to die. Until Paris was liberated, Rolf used his influence to save hundreds of Jews in order to make Anna happy. Rolf never completely abandoned his racist ideas, but he loved and protected Anna for forty-nine years until he died at age seventy-one in the couple's house in Paris.

"He was a strange man," says Anna. "But he never would lift a finger to hurt anyone, Jew or gentile. And he risked everything to protect me and to help many others because he loved me with all his heart." Declares Anna, "He saved me and took care of me for practically my entire life, and for that I truly love him."

Prescription for Love

~

Shauwna robbed thousands of dollars from her parents' checking account and ran away from her Pittsburgh home swearing to never return. The nineteen-year-old troubled teen disappeared without a trace.

Remarkably, her dad, Richard, wasn't mad but worried sick over what had led his baby girl to such a hurtful and desperate act. "The money didn't matter," says Richard. "Not that it wasn't a lot of money, but she was more important to me. I just wanted to know why she did it. What did we do wrong and how could we help her? From the second she was born I loved her more than anything in the world."

Shauwna was Richard and Marta's only child, and they loved their daughter in the only way they knew how—with all their hearts. They never spoiled her, and they always spent time with Shauwna, taking her on trips and getting involved in her school and cheerleading activities. But by the time she was fourteen, she started getting in trouble, dating a twenty-one-year-old man behind her parents' backs and getting drunk every weekend. "When we found out, we were out of our minds," says Marta. "We just weren't prepared for that so early in her life. We didn't know what to do. It really broke our hearts to see her hurting herself that way. We spent so much time with her trying to help, but nothing worked."

By the time she was seventeen, Shauwna had already been arrested twice for possession of cocaine and been suspended from school over a dozen times for everything from drugs to fighting to even indecent exposure when she was caught having sex in the bathroom with her boyfriend. Nothing her parents did, from punishing to talking to sending her away to live with her grandmother one summer proved helpful. She only grew more unruly with every passing year.

But her parents loved her unconditionally, even when she graduated from high school and told them she didn't need their college money because she wasn't going. "That was really frustrating," says Richard. "She didn't want to do anything to help herself. She just wanted to hang out with her drug-addict friends and a bunch of older guys, half of which I could only guess were dealers. But we wouldn't kick her out. We didn't want to cut off her only lifeline to a healthy world."

Then came the final blow to their hearts. When Marta gave her a check to sign up for a cosmetology class, she changed the amount on the check to $10,000 and cleaned out her parents' checking account. Then she ran away. "I was so happy when she told me about the cosmetology class," says Marta. "I didn't care what she did, I just wanted her to be fulfilled and she seemed excited about it. So when she did this, I couldn't even believe it."

Her father was more hurt than shocked. "I knew in her state of mind she was definitely capable of that kind of act," explains Richard. "But it still hurt—like someone took a shovel and hit me in the head. She did a lot of crazy things. But that was the first time she ever stole from us and then vanished. It was like a nightmare."

Then came a vicious letter in the mail. A simple note in her handwriting read, "Bye, bye! Leave me alone!" Her parents were devastated. "That really broke our hearts," says Marta. "All we ever tried to do was help." Though friends and family all advised them to notify the police, the doctor and his wife refused. "I wasn't going to send my daughter to jail," says Richard. "That's not what she needed. But I was convinced that now she needed us more than ever. She was so confused but at least at home we could try and help her until she got her act together. But out there alone she was prey to anything or anyone. We just wanted her to be safe."

That's when the fifty-two-year-old M.D. made the monumental decision: he'd sell his practice and devote his life to finding and helping his daughter. "Medicine was such an important part of my life," recalls Richard. "But my daughter and my family were my life, and I was prepared to do whatever I had to do to help them."

He immediately hired a slew of private detectives and personally traveled to ten different cities in the first six months of his search, distributing his daughter's photo from bars to police stations in search of any clues as to where his daughter had vanished. Meanwhile, Shauwna had used a dozen different names in cities from New York to Los Angeles, making it nearly impossible to track her. "I wasn't getting very far," says Richard. "And my wife and I weren't having much of a life ourselves because of it. But she understood that I would never give up. When you love a little girl, you don't stop; you can't. If it took me the rest of my life I would have kept looking to make sure she was all right. If I found her, and she was living a happy life, I promised myself and my wife I wouldn't bother her."

The first real leads on Shauwna's whereabouts came from a police station in Salt Lake City after more than two years of searching. Shauwna had been detained and released for suspicion of solicitation. But since she kept moving from place to place it wasn't much help. "She never stayed in the same place for very long," says Richard. "Whenever I'd get close to her, she'd vanish again. It was so frustrating."

Richard ran television, radio and newspaper ads across the country and spoke on radio talk shows from coast to coast. The doctor spent five years and a fortune on his tireless pursuit. When the couple ran out of money, they took out a mortgage on their house to fund their search. "I didn't care if it put us in the poorhouse," says Richard. "I was going to make sure she was all right."

Soon Richard was spending almost five or six days a week searching for his daughter. "He wouldn't give up even when I was tempted to," reveals Marta. "He just loved her so much. When I married him I knew he would be the most loving father. And I was right."

Almost six years later, a break finally came with a call from a priest in Albuquerque, New Mexico. He'd heard Richard on the radio and thought a recent confession he heard might be Shauwna. "He wouldn't violate the confidentiality of the confession by telling me what she confessed," explains Richard, "but he said it sounded like my daughter's scenario. But more importantly he felt she was on the verge of doing something desperate."

Richard immediately flew to Albuquerque with a private investigator and the two staked out the area near the church where Shauwna was suspected to be. "This was the closest I'd ever been," says Richard. "I had a feeling this was it, but I was scared about what the priest had said about her being in trouble. My worst fear was we would get to her too late."

For a week, he and the investigator combed the streets of Albuquerque from the bars to strip clubs to the crack houses and flophouses and cheap apartments. Finally they struck gold! A local bartender knew Shauwna—she had worked as a cocktail waitress for a while but was fired for showing up strung out on drugs two weeks earlier, the same day she saw the priest. Since then the bartender hadn't seen her. But he did have an address.

Richard and his investigator rushed over to the run-down pay-by-the-week hotel with Shauwna's photo. She was still living there, but the landlord hadn't seen her come out of her apartment in a few days. "She thought she was probably out of town or something," says Richard. After convincing the landlord he was Shauwna's father, she agreed to let the two men into her apartment.

There lying on the bed in the ramshackle room was his darling daughter, emaciated beyond recognition, remnants of cocaine and an empty bottle of pills on the bed next to her. "She wasn't breathing, and she barely had a pulse," says Richard. "I was terrified. It occurred to me that we might find her dead, but never that we'd find her like that and be moments from losing her."

Richard immediately performed rescue breathing on his daughter until he heard her gasp for air. Then they threw her in the car and rushed her to the hospital three blocks away while he slapped her hands and shook her, all the time talking to her. "I just kept saying, 'I love you,' over and over into her ear," recalls Richard. "I was crying, and I just couldn't face losing her just when I had found her." Speeding through stoplights, they made it to the hospital in under two minutes.

With tears streaming down his face and his medical ID out, he ran into the emergency room with his little girl in his arms. "I know she was moments away from dying," says Richard. "I was sure of it." ER doctors and nurses went to work pumping Shauwna's stomach. Finally, an hour later, Richard's little girl came to. "She woke up and just looked at me, and we both started crying," says Richard. "And then she said she was sorry and that she loved me. It was about ten years since the last time I had heard her say anything like that. I just lost it; I was so happy."

Her father's endless devotion to finding his little girl did much more than save Shauwna's life—it gave her the courage and faith to make a new and better life for herself. After getting out of the hospital, Shauwna flew back to Pittsburgh with her father, where she agreed to enroll in a local drug treatment program, and she and her parents began weekly family counseling sessions. In order to help her get back on her feet physically, her father prescribed a diet and exercise program for her, which he worked on closely with her every day.

Less than a year later, Shauwna was accepted into college and took a job working part-time in a hospital. And today she's a successful special education teacher with a wonderful fiancé and a great life ahead of her. But not a day goes by that she doesn't call Richard and tell him he's the best dad on earth.

Love Is Thicker Than Bullets

～

*I*n 1991, when, along with Slovenia, the Yugoslavian Republic of Croatia declared its independence from Yugoslavia, Edin was just a normal
nine-year-old girl growing up in the Croatian district of
Vukovar. The next day Croatian Serb rebels sympathetic
to Yugoslavia attacked a police station in the central
Croatian area of Krajina. Two months later those rebels
were joined by the Yugoslavian National Army in a massive attack on Vukovar and a full-scale war was at hand.

Thousands fled and hundreds died while less than one
thousand Croatian National Guardsmen and police
along with one thousand volunteers defended the city
during the three-month siege by the massive Yugoslavian

army, the fourth largest military force in Europe. Edin's parents faced the difficult decision to stay and fight or flee. "We did not want to desert our people," remembers Edin's father, Lavoslav, who together with his wife, Ana, ran a small café in the city. "We had been under fire for so long, we didn't know when the end would come or what would happen next. But we had so much to care for in our city—our home, our restaurant and our friends and family who all lived in Vukovar. But we were most concerned about our daughter's safety."

Aware of the danger but unprepared to flee, they sent Edin off to their cousin in Italy so she could catch a plane to the United States where Edin's aunt lived. The plan was that when all was well again her parents would send for her.

As the city was pounded by artillery one night, innocent little Edin was about to begin an adventure that would change her life forever. A treacherous two-day journey sent Edin to Venice, Italy, where she boarded a plane to Washington, D.C. But before she left, Edin made a remarkable promise. "She was getting in the jeep and she looked back and said, 'I love you, Poppa, and I promise I will help,' " remembers Lavoslav. "I told her not to worry—to leave that to us."

As the war waged on Vukovar became a city in ruin. The only real contact with the outside world was word of mouth from refugees who escaped. Finally, on November 18, 1991, the city fell to the mighty forces of the Yugoslav National Army. Many were killed and tortured and thousands were rounded up and taken to prison camps or detained. Edin's parents were thrown into a makeshift detention center where daily tortures were commonplace, and the prisoners were starved in hopes of slow death.

Meanwhile, Edin was doing well in Washington, D.C. Her aunt and uncle took great care of her while they all watched the situation in Croatia worsen on television. The ongoing crises afforded Edin refugee status. But Edin hadn't spoken to her parents or even heard word of them in over two months and she was heartbroken. Despite her guardians' attempts to take her mind off her parents, Edin wanted to take action.

Though they did not tell Edin, Lavoslav's sister, Kat, believed her brother was already dead. "We had heard some things from a refugee about how the area of the city where Lavoslav owned his shop had been hardest hit," says Kat. "We didn't want to tell Edin yet, but in the middle of all this she walks in the door and says, 'I'm going to rescue Momma and Poppa.' I didn't know what she was talking about."

Little did they know that Edin, who only spoke English as a second language, had started a letter-writing campaign with the help of a friend. The campaign would soon become an avalanche of attempts to find her parents. Over the next few months, while her parents clung to life in a dank and dark interrogation camp a world away, Edin literally wrote hundreds of letters to everyone from President Clinton and the United Nations to even the President of Yugoslavia begging for help to find her parents. "We had no idea what she was doing," says her aunt Kat. "But she kept telling us how she was going to find her mom and dad."

Incredibly, only one month after her first letters went out, she was getting responses from the U.S. State Department and the White House. Remembers Edin, "The first letters I got were all telling me everything was being done that could be. They were not real letters. So I just kept writing."

For every courtesy letter she received, she wrote two more to the same person. After another month and over two hundred and fifty letters, she received a phone call from the U.S. State Department that startled her aunt. "They wanted to know who was really writing these letters for her," says Kat. "They didn't believe that it was her, but maybe an adult who just wanted to use her to get attention. When she got on the phone and they heard how determined she was, they finally believed it was her and they wanted to meet her." Officials extended an invitation to Edin to meet with them to help her better understand all that was being done to resolve the situation in Croatia.

Edin's attempts began to get noticed as the rest of the world was finally taking notice of Croatia. United Nations negotiators were working out a cease-fire agreement between Yugoslavia and Croatia. But Edin was determined to work out her own negotiations and she continued to write her letters. Government officials were soon phoning Edin on a weekly basis. "It was incredible," says Kat. "We were finding out more from Edin than our sources in Croatia."

But Edin didn't just want to be informed—she wanted action. "I wanted to know where my parents were and when I could go back," says Edin. "I promised to help." As negotiations dragged on for a cease-fire and subsequent end to hostilities, officials assured Edin the situation would be resolved soon, and only then could they look for her parents.

Meanwhile, her parents were lucky to still be alive. "Fortunately we were not being tortured or killed like so many others," says Lavoslav. "But they were letting us die slowly. We had nothing but scraps to eat for months. But we were both strong and held on for Edin and for each other and the one day when we would all be reunited. We knew it would come."

Finally, on January 2, 1992, Croatia and Yugoslavia signed a truce in Sarajevo. But the death and destruction were far from over. The city of Vukovar had been demolished, and Edin's parents were still being imprisoned in the conquered territory. As Yugoslav officials denied inhumane treatment of POWs and residents of captured territories, Edin kept begging them to find her parents. Amazingly, her parents' names soon appeared on a list of Vukovar prisoners that the Yugoslavs would release and hand over to the UN forces in order to show good faith and to certify that prisoners of war were being treated fairly under Yugoslav occupation. "The UN asked the Yugoslavs to locate certain individuals who were suspected of being in prison or dead to determine if there was criminal treatment by the Yugoslavs or not," explains Lavoslov. "I know that it was no coincidence that our names appeared on that list—it was because of Edin."

As UN forces prepared to move into Croatia, allegations increased about prison camps and genocide. The Yugoslav National Army did their best to cooperate with international authorities in order to avoid international suspicion and opposition. And Edin's parents were suddenly turned over to UN forces. "One day some of the soldiers came and grabbed me," explains Lavoslav. "I thought of course I was to be shot or tortured. I was blindfolded and put into a truck. Then I heard my wife's voice. The next thing I knew we were being released. It was all like a dream."

United States officials agree that Edin's sincere dedication definitely helped her parents. "Edin's persistence made people down here stand up and take notice," says an unnamed State Department insider. "Her parents would have probably been lost in the shuffle if it weren't for her. That's just the way it is when you have a war situation and thousands of people missing."

As UN troops and a slew of foreign journalists began moving into the area they found shocking evidence of mass executions and many atrocities against humanity, including the execution of several hundred civilians and wounded patients from a Vukovar area hospital.

Within three months Edin's parents were granted the right to enter the United States to be with their daughter. "She told us all that she had a feeling her parents would be coming home for her birthday," remembers her aunt. "And she was right!" Two days before her birthday Edin got her wish. As they met their daughter at the airport, she ran into her father's arms and wouldn't let go. "She was so excited she knocked me over," says Lavoslav. "I had lost quite a bit of weight since I'd seen her last, and I was a little weak. But though my body was weak, my heart was strong."

Nowadays the reunited family lives happily in Maryland, worlds away from the death and destruction of Vukovar. But Edin's parents will never forget the incredible lifesaving love of a little girl that made the reunion possible. "She did something that can hardly be believed and never forgotten," rejoiced Lavoslav. "She is our treasure and we will always love her and cherish her."

Brotherly Love

———

*B*attling brothers Jeff and Brad spent their whole lives despising each other. And it seemed that nothing and no one could bring them together. "I hated my brother—I mean I *really* hated him!" says Jeff. "The only thing we ever saw eye to eye on from the time we were kids was that we couldn't stand each other, and that we both loved our younger sister, Adrian."

The two boys, whose father had left when they were just toddlers, grew up with their mother and baby sister just outside Minneapolis, Minnesota. Less than a year and a half apart in age, they fought like cats and dogs about everything from who would do what chores to who got which toys. "I remember once when I was seven, we fought over this G.I. Joe," recalls Jeff. "We got so crazy we just started ripping it apart, and we destroyed it."

But as the two got older, their feuding grew more dangerous as their fights became more violent. "Through high school we were in fistfights with each other all the time," explains Brad. "We'd even get other kids to help beat each other up. It was unreal. The teachers couldn't believe how we could do that."

Their mom, Evelyn, tried everything she could from talking to the children to punishing them to even taking them to a child psychiatrist. But nothing could calm their fury. "One psychiatrist said that we both were convinced that our mom loved the other one more," says Jeff. "Another one said we both blamed the other for our father leaving. But I don't know that either one of us thought like that. We just thought the other one was weird and hated each other."

By the time they were eighteen, their fights were all-out brawls, frequently forcing their mom to call the police to break them up. The final blow came on Brad's high school graduation day when Jeff insulted his younger brother in front of his girlfriend. "I was jealous because I liked her," admits Jeff. "So I told her he was a loser who didn't deserve her. We started shouting at each other, then all of a sudden I saw Brad come at me with a bat. That's when things really got scary. Looking back, I don't think he would have actually hit me with it. But at the time I thought he would."

Fearing Brad's attack, Jeff grabbed a Coke bottle that was on the table and cracked Brad across the face with it. The fierce blow knocked Brad to his knees and the shattered glass cut a deep gash next to his eye. While Jeff stood stunned at what he had done, an enraged, bleeding Brad slowly rose to his feet and whacked his brother with all his might in the stomach with the bat. As Jeff fell down he reached up and pulled his brother down with him. And soon the two were both grappling on the ground, punching, kicking and scratching each other. The deadly showdown didn't end until both brothers just lay there, one with several broken ribs and the other a concussion.

Their injuries would heal in just a few weeks, but the damage to the family would last for decades. "I can remember my mom screaming and everything," says Jeff. "The next thing I knew I woke up in the hospital, and I asked if my brother was all right. They said he was OK, and that was the last time I ever even talked about him for twenty years."

When the two boys were released from the hospital, Brad went to stay with his girlfriend, and Jeff went back to college. They both decided never to speak to or see each other again. Despite all of their mom's and their sister's efforts to bring about a reconciliation, the two brothers remained apart in every way. "We knew we were breaking our mom's and sister's hearts," says Jeff. "But I guess we were just too caught up in our own anger to care."

Brad went on to become a lieutenant in the Army and fought bravely in the Gulf War, while Jeff became a financial advisor for a management firm. They both married and each had a boy and a girl. But they lived totally separate lives, Jeff in Sacramento, California, and Brad outside of Atlanta, Georgia. Meanwhile, their sister became a missionary after graduating from college and spent fifteen years in Africa working to help the hungry and diseased children of the continent's impoverished countries. The brothers arranged visits with their mom and sister so as never to cross paths.

But on Christmas 1996, a phone call from their mother would bring them into each other's presence for the first time in two decades when they learned their sister was dying of leukemia. "I was just about to pick up the phone to call my sister and wish her merry Christmas," remembers Jeff, "when I get this call from Mom telling me Adrian was in the hospital." Jeff and Brad both rushed back to Minneapolis and over to the hospital. "It was the first time I didn't even worry about whether my brother would be there or not," says Brad.

Meanwhile, in the hospital their sister lay in a bed in

Intensive Care connected to a slew of machines testing her blood and feeding her. She was weak and frail. "We both got there at the same time," recalls Brad. "And at first we both were a little stunned at how much the other had changed in twenty years, and then I remembered all that rage coming right back again. But then I just focused on sis and I guess he did too. I hated him and wished he wasn't there, but I loved my sister more than life and I kept that at the front of my mind."

As they both stood by the bed, their sister and mother just stared at them, forgetting for a moment that Adrian was deathly ill. "I guess seeing us together like that side by side just was such a shock, it was hard to swallow," says Brad. "So they just kept on staring."

The doctors informed Adrian's family that she was in a very advanced stage of leukemia. Apparently she had begun showing symptoms of the disease years earlier but ignored it while serving in Africa. Now only the most drastic and aggressive treatment could save her. She would begin powerful chemotherapy and radiation treatments the next day. If the treatments didn't work, she would have at the most a few months left to live. "We were all in the room together when the doctors told us that real straightforward," remembers Brad. "They didn't even try to sugarcoat it at all. It was just straight up—she's dying! I was speechless. I remember looking at Jeff and seeing tears welling up in his eyes."

But despite their sister's desperate situation, the two men had no intention of letting this family challenge bring them back together. "We both were trying very hard not to look at each other," says Jeff. "We knew we both had to be there to care for our sister, and that was it. Whenever I tell this story people always expect that we just would have bonded there in the hospital like in a movie or something, but it just wasn't going to happen."

But as both brothers fawned over their beloved sister while secretly spewing venom for each other, Adrian revealed her master plan for a miracle. Over the next few weeks while she underwent her painful treatments, she asked only one thing from her family—that both her brothers stay with her and pretend to love each other. "She got the strangest look on her face all of a sudden and looked up at us both and said, 'Just playact until I die or I'm better, and it will be the best gift you ever gave me.'" Both brothers glared at each other at the mere suggestion of such a reconciliation. "As selfish as it sounds now," recalls Brad, "I thought, and I think he did too, about telling her that was ridiculous and walking out of the room. I was there for her, but I hated my brother and couldn't imagine pretending to love him. But in a split second, we both said yes."

Both brothers agreed to a temporary truce for the sister they loved, yet they were sure to clarify that this was just an act. "I remember we met out in the hall and literally made a deal that we would act like we really loved each other in front of her," says Jeff. "We even worked out what we'd say and how we'd do it. But we both knew it was just an act."

The brothers moved into their mother's house temporarily. And over the course of the next several weeks, they did whatever they could to show their sister they were keeping their promise—talking, playing cards at her bedside, watching TV together—whatever it took to fill her with joy.

"It was funny because I think we even tried to be competitive at loving each other," says Brad, "trying to show that we were each better at it than the other."

As Adrian grew weaker and weaker with the painful but necessary treatments, she was bolstered only by her brothers' commitment to their promise of love. Every time the nurses would bring her back to her room after a treatment session, Brad and Jeff were waiting for her together with big smiles on their faces and a new batch of hospital jokes to tell her. Within minutes her tears would turn to laughter. Once they even performed a funny hospital sketch to get her mind off the pain. Just seeing her brothers have so much fun with each other healed her heart.

But her body was not responding, and within one month doctors were losing hope as the leukemia rapidly advanced. "It was clear to us that they didn't think she was going to make it," says Jeff. Faced with the cruel reality that their sister was going to die, Jeff and Brad both made all the arrangements necessary to stay in Minneapolis with Adrian until the end and make her as happy and comfortable as they could. "I remember after we made all the plans, my brother and I hugged each other, and I could tell we both really meant it. We held each other a long time and we both kind of teared up a little."

Two and a half weeks later on an unusually warm and sunny winter's day, Adrian died. But before she passed, she thanked her family, then looked at her brothers and asked for one last favor. "She said, 'Keep it up, guys,' " recalls Jeff. "Then she just shut her eyes. She died a few hours later."

The day after her funeral, while sitting at the dinner table in their mother's house, Brad and Jeff talked over a cup of coffee of how they would try and respect their sister's last wishes. They agreed that the past was the past, and decided neither owed the other any apologies for mistakes they both made when they were just children. "We agreed that the best thing we could do was just put all that stuff behind us," says Brad, "just forget any of it ever happened because otherwise we'd get in the same silly arguments all over again."

The reunited brothers decided to get to know each

other all over again—this time as adults and friends instead of sibling rivals. "We weren't promising anything was going to come of it," says Jeff, "but we agreed that we'd give it a shot. You know, talking on the phone every couple of weeks or so and maybe even getting together once every couple of months with our families."

Amazingly, since their sister's death, the two brothers have become best friends. Despite living on opposite ends of the country, they bring their families together three or four times a year for get-togethers and have even started their own company together. Before their mother died a few years ago of cancer, she told them their friendship had made her life complete.

They have never fought again, and every year on their sister's birthday they get together to celebrate their new relationship and thank her for the new happiness she gave them. "There isn't anything I wouldn't do for my brother now, and I know he feels the same way about me," says Jeff. "And none of this would have ever happened if it wasn't for Adrian. I lost my sister, but before she left this world she gave me back my brother and there's no greater gift she could have given me."

Jokes Brad, "I love that guy like a brother. I know I should have felt that way a long time ago. But now I really do."

No Such Thing as Too Much Love!

~~~~~

*I*t was 1995 when ten children plus their five cousins were living in a one-bedroom roach-infested apartment huddled amid their own feces, baby's vomit and a slew of empty soda cans and potato chip wrappers. From four different fathers, the abandoned clan of children—the youngest a newborn boy and the oldest a fourteen-year-old boy—had been left by their alcoholic mother to fend for themselves while she wandered in and out on binges.

All abused in one way or another by the many strangers that came and went in their lives, the lice-infested children were barely surviving, and it was a life hardly worth living. The oldest, Frank, would steal food to feed his younger brothers and sisters, while his sister Asucena hadn't been to school in years, as she hopelessly took on the role of mom, trying to cook and care for the other children in whatever way she could.

Then one day an anonymous phone call to the police notified them of the children's condition, sending officers to the scene to take the children into protective custody. "That's when we read about them in the local paper," says Van. "It was such a sad story that you just couldn't help wanting to do something. But at that time we never thought we could be the ones to save all those kids."

Navy chief Van and his wife, Shirley, who was working as a court clerk, were getting ready to settle into a comfortable retirement as the last of their own children left the house. But as the Arizona couple lay together in bed one night, they heard a strange and disturbing sound, which made them think twice about what they wanted—it was the sound of silence. "Our two children were finally out on their own, and the place was just too quiet," recalls Van. "I couldn't even get to sleep that night, it felt so lonely. So I turned to my wife and asked her if she was asleep. She said she couldn't sleep also because of the quiet. So I said why don't we think about adopting a child?"

Shirley immediately began researching how the couple could first become foster parents to try things out. The next thing they knew they had two foster children. "It was a wonderful feeling," remembers Shirley with the fondness of a new mom. "We really fell in love with these first two kids, and so one thing led to another and they gave us three more." While permanent homes were soon found for their first two foster children, their love and commitment to helping unknowingly brought them three new foster children from the family they had read about in the papers. "We didn't know that these were those kids until after we got them," says Van. "Then we started to meet the whole clan little by little, and we started really growing attached to them."

First three-year-old Stephanie, then her brothers Jose and Juan—it was love at first sight for Van and Shirley. "I can't tell you what those little hearts did to us," says Shirley. "From the moment they came into our lives and gave us their trust and love, we knew what we wanted in life; we wanted to adopt them. My heart just told me it was the right thing to do." Soon after that, the local Department of Economic Security asked them to take two more of the siblings as foster children, and Doni and Veronica were added to the fold. That meant there were five little sets of feet running around the house— enough to drive any parent crazy, but the couple did their best. "We loved all these kids," says Van. "But it was definitely more than we ever expected. We figured eventually we would adopt a few of them and make it official—but not all of them." While Van and Shirley took care of their five foster children, they started to see five other faces wandering in and out of the house—those of the other five siblings who were all scattered in other foster homes.

That's when DES workers, ecstatic over how well-adjusted and happy the five foster children were with Van and Shirley, asked them to make the final decision to adopt not just one or two of the children but all of them. "Though we had thought of adopting a child, five was just a little too much for us," says Shirley. "We just didn't know if we could handle raising all these children. I mean, we weren't kids anymore, and this was a lot of work. We had to say no."

But in March 1997, when caseworkers informed them the ten children would be split up between two adoptive families, one in Michigan, the other in the East, Van saw ten hearts he'd fallen in love with breaking, and it was a thought he couldn't bear. Van and Shirley realized exactly what they had to do.

"The thought of splitting up this family like that really tugged at my heart," says Van. "They belonged together and we wanted to help make sure of that. We really loved these kids. Our hearts made the decision for us. And we knew the love they gave us could make anything possible." Van and Shirley knew the only way to keep them together, so they made the incredible decision to adopt not just their five foster kids but the whole kit and caboodle of ten kids! The only question that remained was whether or not the children wanted to be adopted. So they gathered all ten children together for a giant pizza party and popped the question. "They all agreed," says Shirley. "But Juan broke down and cried when he realized he would never go back to his mom. He was grieving and my heart broke for him. I held him and hugged him. We assured him that if she ever sobered up the kids could see her."

But there was still the matter of how they would take care of this battalion of boys and girls and how they would be able to afford it. Van quit the Navy to have more time for the kids and took a job as a part-time security guard close to home. "I loved the Navy like a family," says Van. "But I loved these kids even more. They were now the most important thing in my life. I did whatever I had to do to protect them."

Now Van and Shirley's new family isn't too different from any other family—just multiplied! They spend $1500 a month on groceries, they shop at Wal-Mart, all the kids have bikes and eight have braces. The children all get allowances, and they are all expected to do chores. "I want these kids to have every opportunity," says the devoted dad. Meanwhile, Shirley's day is now nonstop. She wakes up at the crack of dawn every day and prepares breakfast for her company of kids. Then she becomes a bus driver. "By the time I'm done dropping off all the kids at their different schools at different times, it's time to start picking up the young ones." By about 4 P.M. she's done and then it's time to start cooking dinner. Then she helps with homework and does the laundry and household chores. But it's all a labor of love. "I realized just how much I loved them, and my mothering instinct has really kicked in. I can't tell you how it feels to have a seventeen-year-old boy give you a hug, or a seventeen-year-old girl open up to you after what they have been through. There's no retirement that could give me the blessings I receive from these children every day. They deserve all the love I can give them. You don't have to talk, you just listen. And you get filled up."

Now the couple, who have been married thirty-one years, says they are looking forward to a whole lot of grandchildren. "Can you imagine all the love we are going to have here," exclaims Van. "We'll certainly never be lonely again." Meanwhile, Van says if he won the lottery tomorrow he'd adopt a whole new slew of kids. "I'd take all the kids I could because you cannot have or give enough love. If this is a miracle, it's the kids' love that made it happen. Our hearts overruled our minds. We might give them a lot of love but we get a whole lot more back, and that's more important than anything else we could have in our retirement."

Never Give Up!

~

*K*eith, a successful Los Angeles–area businessman, was on a routine sales call when tragedy
turned his life upside down. On a sunny California day
he was driving along a busy boulevard when in the blink
of an eye another driver crossed the center lane and hit
Keith's car head-on.

The severe crash left Keith with serious brain damage
and severed nerves. Called brain shearing, the condition
left him unable to walk, talk, speak, sit up, breathe or
swallow on his own. Doctors said even if he emerged
from his coma, he would never regain any real quality
of life. "The doctors were sure he wouldn't make it,"
remembers his wife, Marilyn. "They were ready to give

up on him. They recommended that if he went into cardiac arrest not to resuscitate him. I was completely destroyed. It was awful. You want to have hope, but they just keep telling you that it doesn't look like there's any."

Soon after arriving in the hospital Keith's breathing functions returned, but the doctors still refused to predict any recovery. Marilyn wouldn't accept the hospital's pessimistic prognosis, and she was determined to help her husband however she could in the anticipation that one day he would return to her. Recalls Marilyn, "There was no way I was going to give up on my husband—not ever."

Marilyn inspired her own faith and courage by reminding herself of the man she loved, the man she remembered him being. All those wonderful, beautiful memories helped remind her how he used to light up her life, and how now it was her turn to help bring him back.

"He was the most energetic and loving man around," says Marilyn. "He grew up in an adoptive family because his own family deserted him, but he bore no grudge. He still loved his family, all of them. He was so full of life and love for everyone. I knew now I had to be full of that life and love for him. I was going to see him through."

Every day, Marilyn stayed by her husband's side and spoke to him constantly as he lingered in his hospital bed seemingly lifeless. She bought countless books on how to wake people from comas, and tried whatever she could to excite his senses. "I did everything imaginable from propping him up with pillows to rubbing his hands, combing his hair, anything," says Marilyn. "I'd put a telephone to his ear and say talk. I'd read books to him and do things to irritate him hoping it might wake him up."

But no matter how much faith Marilyn had, it seemed as if nothing would work. And the more she tried to believe, it seemed the harder the hospital fought to convince her that her husband was a hopeless cause. "Once we even asked the hospital for smelling salts to see if that would help, but they said they didn't have any. Can you imagine a hospital saying they didn't have any smelling salts? That's how much they had given up on my Keith."

Finally even Marilyn's unshakable faith was tested one day when she propped her husband's head up for the umpteenth time, and he just sat there motionless as if he was dead already. "All the doctors were telling me he'd never come back," remembers the devoted wife. "And I when I looked at him just sitting there like that I began to think that if he was going to be that way the rest of his life, it might not be worth it. But I couldn't give up."

As the days and weeks dragged on, doctors became even more convinced that Keith would never regain consciousness, let alone have any real sense of who he was before the accident. But despite the doctors' lack of faith, Marilyn felt driven by what she could only describe as the feeling that her husband's spirit was still in there somewhere trying to reach out to her. So she kept trying anything and everything she thought might help. Marilyn would not be denied her right to try and save her husband, but she was reaching the end of her rope. "I was really running out of ideas," recalls Marilyn. "But then I thought I needed to give him something that would inspire him to come back."

Ever hopeful but discouraged, she brought a picture of the happy couple embracing at a nearby lake in better times to the hospital. She held up the photo to her husband's eyes hoping for some response. "I figured maybe I could see him blink or move his eyes or something," explains Marilyn. "I wasn't hoping for much, just any small sign."

What she received was nothing short of a miracle! All of a sudden, Keith emerged from his coma, opened his eyes, then reached up and took the picture in his hand and pulled it toward him. Then in one swift, incredible motion raised the magical photograph to his lips and kissed it affectionately. "I was blown away," says Marilyn. "It was the first real sign we had and what a sign. I knew at that moment all the doctors were wrong."

But amazingly, despite the dramatic reaction, doctors

were still unwilling to accept there was hope for a significant recovery. "They tried telling me that this was just some kind of involuntary reaction—that it didn't mean anything. I thought they were being ridiculous. There may have been brain damage, but my husband was still in there. I knew I could bring him back."

Marilyn was more sure than ever that the doctors were wrong. Though her husband's brain damage made it difficult to be certain whether he was actually conscious or not, she knew he was back. Inspired by her husband's act, Marilyn became unstoppable. She stepped up all her efforts to reach her husband and rehabilitate him. And he came through for her. "From then on out he was responding to just about everything I'd do," remembers Marilyn. "I put a brush up to his head and he started combing his hair. Then I put a toothbrush in his hand and he raised it to his mouth. Then I gave him a pen and he started to write. I knew these were not just reactions!"

Finally, doctors had no choice but to accept that Keith was slowly returning and could be rehabilitated, yet they had no way of explaining the recovery. "I've seen people wake up from comas after a week or two," said one doctor. "But he was out for six weeks."

More than a year later Keith is still piecing together who he was. He is learning to walk, talk and live life all over again. But one thing he doesn't need to learn is the power of his wife's love for him.

"Recovering from brain damage is a slow road, but we are getting there," says Marilyn. "He's the man I love, and I'll be by his side every step of the way."

A Husband's Sacrifice

~~~

$\mathcal{S}$teven and Francine, a retired middle-class Portland, Oregon, couple, were having marriage trouble. After thirty years together and three children, the only sparks flying were from their tongues when they fought. But they had saved up for years for an adventure Down Under to check out the other side of the world, and they both hoped it might put the pizzazz back in their marriage.

Once there, the feisty fifty-year-olds wanted to see everything from kangaroos to koala bears and especially the man-eating crocodiles. "Ever since my wife saw the *Crocodile Dundee* movies, she wanted to see a crocodile," explains Steven. "And she didn't want to see them in a zoo or something. She wanted them up close."

So they booked a boat tour of some of Australia's well-known wetlands that boasted impressive populations of exotic creatures—and plenty of crocodiles. But when their guide was detained, the adventurous explorers decided to go it alone.

The couple set out on their expedition that morning in a small rented boat, ready for a lazy trip down the river, snapping shots of rare and beautiful birds and maybe even spotting a crocodile or two, all the while referring to their handy guidebook. "It told us what to look out for and what to stay away from," says Steven. "Basically, it said just don't put anything in the water, including yourself, and you would be fine."

It was a perfect day. As they navigated the narrow river, they stared up at the clear blue sky and felt the warm breeze blow and the sun on their backs. They were in heaven—even if they weren't really paying any attention to each other. "This was our dream vacation, and we were really in our own worlds," says Francine. "This was what we had worked so hard for for so many years."

As they made their way around a bend and into a clearing they saw the most amazing sight they had ever beheld—dozens of crocodiles! "Francine screamed," says Steven. "But I reminded her, 'You wanted crocodiles, didn't you?' I figured we'd be okay if we just steered away from them and made our way down the other side of the river."

But suddenly the boat wasn't going where Steven wanted it to. Caught up in some kind of whirlpool, Steven struggled to steer the craft over to the left side of the lake where it was clear, but the current was sending them right toward the crocodiles. Francine panicked, shifting frantically back and forth and sending the boat out of control. "I know now it was the wrong thing to do," says Francine. "But I was going crazy as we got closer. I was so scared!"

All the commotion was attracting the attention of the crocodiles, who were previously motionless. They began rushing toward the boat. "I've never seen anything swim that fast in my life," says Steven. "One second they were a hundred yards away and then they seemed to be right up on us. It was terrifying."

The boat was soon surrounded by the crocodiles, and then the unimaginable happened. As Steven continued to try and bring the boat out of the whirlpool and over to the shoreline, Francine bolted away from the edge and toward the center of the tiny vessel. Her sudden motion rocked the boat violently to one side, throwing her helplessly into the shallow but deadly water. "The whole thing happened so fast," explains Steven, "yet it really did seem like it was going in slow motion at the time. I saw the crocodiles from about ten feet away duck under the second she went into the water. And I knew that was it."

Steven screamed at Francine to rush out of the waist-high water to the shore only a few yards away, but she was frozen with fear. "I was so scared," reveals Francine. "I couldn't move. You know when you are so scared you can't scream. It was like that but I couldn't move." Suddenly Francine felt a snap at her foot and the next thing she knew she was being tossed around like a rag doll. "It was so fast, I couldn't even react. It had me by the ankle and I had no control at that point. It was horrible."

In disbelief Steven watched his beloved wife fight a losing battle to keep her head above water and swim toward the shore while the crocodile pulled her deeper into the water. "I didn't have time to get scared," says Steven. "I knew I had only a second or two to act before it was too late. So I jumped in after her."

Francine was upside down, struggling to keep her head above water. It was only her thick, metal-reinforced high-top hiking boots that were saving her from losing her limb, but it was only a matter of time before the crocodile's razor-sharp teeth broke through the boot.

As Steven lunged beneath the murky water, other crocodiles swirled around the boat. He knew he and Francine were just a few yards from the shore, and if he couldn't save them both, maybe he could at least break Francine free and she could run ashore. "It hit me in

that split second that I would die for her if I had to,"
remembers Steven. "I don't think I ever realized how
much I loved her until that moment."

Unable to see a thing below the water, he scrambled
to feel for Francine's leg. Once he found it, he frantically
worked his hands downward until he felt the tough and
slimy hide of the crocodile's head. Then he poked the
monstrous creature in the eyes as hard as he could. "It
was the only part of his body I could think of that might
be vulnerable," says Steven.

His idea worked! The crocodile immediately released
Francine. But then it twisted its massive body around
and lashed at Steven. "All I saw was that mouth and
those eyes," says Steven. "I just reacted and went for the
eyes again." While the wounded crocodile backed off for
a second, he screamed for his wife to hurry ashore. As
she did, Steven made a break to join her. But then he
felt the mighty power of the crocodile's jaws as its teeth
sank into his arm. "I was just about two or three feet
from the shore when he got me," remembers Steven,
"and my feet were touching bottom so it gave me some
leverage. I somehow just ignored the pain and dragged
the crocodile toward the shore."

Francine watched the grisly sight from the shore as
the crocodile hung from her husband's arm as Steven
stood up out of the water. Steven again frantically poked
at its eyes with his other hand. Miraculously, the croc-

odile let go and dropped away, swimming for the cover of the deeper water. Steven collapsed on the shore. "He was bleeding everywhere," says Francine. "So I dragged him a little farther in, away from the water, and wrapped my shirt around his arm to at least try and stop the bleeding. It was amazing that he still had his arm and I still had my leg!"

As they huddled there alone on the shore, all Francine could think of was her husband's devotion. "I should be dead," says the grateful wife. "The only reason I am alive is his incredible courage and love. He knew when he went into that water that he could die, but he did it anyway to save me. That's true love. He is my knight in shining armor ten times over, and I will never ever forget what he risked for me."

After being rescued Steven and Francine were happy to learn that Steven's arm only needed minor surgery and Francine had only suffered a few cuts and bruises. They resumed their lives back in Oregon, but with one big difference. Now they know a whole lot more about why they've stuck together for so many years and why they will never part. "We really love each other," says Steven. "And I guess it took a crocodile to remind us of that."

Love Won't Steer You Wrong

*I*n over thirty years as a trucker, Roy had never fallen asleep at the wheel. Roy was a Nashville native and became a truck driver when he was eighteen years old, the same year he graduated from high school and married Myrtha, his childhood sweetheart. The happy couple was blessed with three beautiful girls and lived a good solid life in Nashville.

They never went to sleep or hung up the phone angry at each other in more than three decades of wedded bliss, but one night they broke that rule. "We fought because I didn't want to retire," explains Roy. "Years before we agreed I'd get out of the business when I was fifty, but that night I told her how I didn't want to when I called her from the road. Well, she started screaming and hung up on me. She never did that before, so I was pretty ticked. But I just kept driving."

Roy and Myrtha were comfortable but not rich. They had stashed away enough in stocks and mutual funds for a happy retirement. But Roy wasn't ready to park his eighteen wheels just yet. "I still felt young," recalls Roy. "I didn't see why I had to give up the road. I was good at it, and I had fun out there. I always thought havin' that time away from each other probably is why Myrtha and me stuck it out so long."

But his loving wife saw it differently. Thirty years of worrying about her husband was enough for her. And she believed Roy was getting too old for the job—that he needed to rest. "His blood pressure wasn't great, and he was putting on some weight," explains Myrtha. "I wanted him to quit and start taking care of himself."

In fact, Myrtha worried about Roy so much she bought him a cell phone, so he could always call home or call 911 if something happened when he was on the road. "I never knew where he was and if he was all right," says Myrtha. "I mean, I used to lie awake sometimes just imagining all the terrible things that could happen to him out there on the road in the cold and the rain. I didn't know what to think. I was ready to have him here with me. I loved him and I wanted him safe and next to me."

As Roy drove back toward Nashville that night from his last drop in Cincinnati after a weeklong haul out to Los Angeles, the tired trucker struggled to see through blinding snow. It was the wee hour of the morning and one of the worst winters in years. He thought about picking up the cell phone and giving his wife a call, but he was too exhausted. He just wanted to make it home. "It was already real late," says Roy. "And I wanted to sleep in my own bed that night. I really should have pulled over and slept right there, but I just kept moving."

The bad weather, the slick and icy roads, plus the hot air pouring out of his heater quickly intensified his tiredness. He fought hard to stay awake. But it was a losing battle. "I had been doing this for so many years, and I had never fallen asleep," says Roy. "But I knew I was losing it that night. Yet for some reason I just thought I could keep going. I remember thinking maybe my wife was right about me being ready to retire."

As the weather worsened, he grew more and more weary. Occasionally the bright headlights of oncoming traffic revived him for a moment, but the need to squint due to the glare only made him more fatigued and encouraged him to shut his eyes to shield them. "Every time I closed my eyes, it was a little harder to open them back up," remembers Roy. "I felt it coming on strong." Roy knew even a moment of ignoring the road could mean disaster and death. He'd seen friends lose it at the wheel. "I had a buddy jackknife his rig when he conked out at the wheel," reveals Roy. "But I never even came close myself. I really knew I should pull over."

As he contemplated where and when to park, he saw a signpost up ahead. The next accommodations were only ten miles away, and in winter weather checking into a motel would be much safer than pulling alongside the road. Roy decided he'd try and hang on just a few more minutes. "I didn't want to leave the rig on the side of the road in that kind of a storm," says Roy. "With people sliding all over the place on that ice, I thought somebody could lose control and slam into me. And since it was so close I thought I would just go on ahead a few more miles."

As Roy struggled to stay alert, he thought of how much he loved his wife, and how sorry he was he ever argued about not wanting to retire. "I kept thinking about how she was saying I was getting too old for this. I thought of how I'd be letting her down if I let anything happen. But I was just so tired all of a sudden."

As the road up ahead became a big blur of snow and sleet, Roy's mind wandered to his wife and he felt a warm feeling come over his whole body. He felt like he was on a cool beach in the sun. Then the unimaginable happened—he fell asleep at the wheel! "I just felt so good all of a sudden. I was having a great dream."

As his hands dropped, they turned the steering wheel

to the left, sending the eighteen-wheeler drifting left of the center lane and into oncoming traffic. But despite the squeal of the wheels Roy only fell deeper into sleep. "I must have really been out of it," says Roy. "I was dreaming about my wife and how she wanted me to stop driving. And she just kept telling me in my dream how much she loved me and missed me out there on the road."

As Roy drifted deeper and deeper into slumber, the cruise control kept the massive vehicle rolling full-speed toward disaster. Though it had been only a few moments since he'd fallen asleep, it was long enough to send him almost completely to the other side of the road. In the thick snow and wind it would be virtually impossible for an oncoming driver to react in time to avoid disaster once he noticed Roy's truck barreling toward him.

Then the worst happened. Another trucker was headed right toward Roy, unable to see his lights through the bad weather. And they were only seconds apart. But Roy was fast asleep. "I just kept dreaming I was back at home with my wife," says Roy. "She was telling me she loved me and not to go back on the road. I finally agreed, and then in my dream I heard the phone ringing in the house."

But the ringing phone was real. It was the cell phone his wife had given him in case of an emergency. Myrtha was calling to check up on him. "I was feeling real bad about hanging up on him," remembers Myrtha. "I mean, I thought I was right, but I knew he needed my support when he was out there, so I figured I'd call him and tell him I loved him."

The loud shrill of the ring finally awakened Roy just in time to see the oncoming truck headed straight for him. "All I saw were bright lights coming right toward me," remembers Roy. "It was the most terrifying moment I have ever had in my entire life. I thought I was going to die."

Roy quickly pumped the brakes and instantly jerked the wheel to the right. The other driver did the same and the two trucks ditched on opppsite sides of the road, Roy's trailer spilling over onto its side. "I couldn't believe I was alive," recalls Roy. "And that I wasn't even hurt was a miracle. So then I looked to see the other truck, and I saw the driver getting out and coming over to me so I knew he was all right, too."

Roy composed himself, then answered the cell phone, which amazingly was still ringing. "It was my wife calling," says Roy with a smile. "She just wanted to say she loved me and she wanted to know if I was all right. I swear I just started laughing, I was so happy to hear her voice. I told her I was fine. I didn't want to worry her until I got home and she knew I was safe."

Skid marks on the road would later show that at their closest point the two trucks were only a few feet apart.

Roy called the highway patrol and soon a tow truck was dispatched and a trooper brought Roy back home. He immediately woke Myrtha and told her the horrific tale, then let her know he was finally home for good. "I didn't know whether to laugh or cry," says Myrtha. "But I threw my arms around him and told him he was damned right he was done with trucking."

Now Roy says he has a new occupation. "My job now is to love my wife more than anything else in the world—even truckin'. And that's just fine with me."

Unconditional Love

*K*iley was only ten when she first felt the call of the catwalk after watching an episode of *Star Search* on TV. "The winner had such nice clothes, and everybody was clapping for her and looking up at her," recalls Kiley. "I wanted to be perfect just like that." But her strict parents wouldn't hear of any modeling career for Kiley. They wanted her to go to college, meet a nice man and settle down and get married and have kids. "They wanted me to be like one of the *The Brady Bunch* kids or something," says Kiley. "I just wanted to have fun with my life. I wanted some action, and I wanted to get out of this town."

She grew up in the suburbs of Atlanta, Georgia, hundreds of miles from the glamour of New York runways and LA soundstages, but she was determined to one day see her name in lights even though most of her friends thought she was just crazy. The only person she could even talk to about her dreams was a neighbor boy, Kent, a shy and intelligent honor student who had an unrequited crush on Kiley for years. "I always loved Kent because he was my best guy friend," says Kiley. "But I never would have kissed him or anything like that."

When Kiley asked Kent if he'd take her picture so she could send them to local modeling agencies, he was ready and willing. "I'd loved her since we were kids, and I understood what she wanted," says Kent. "I didn't think she was silly. She's beautiful and I knew she could be a model if she wanted to."

An agency expressed some interest in Kiley's pictures and requested she have professional photos taken. So she took a part-time job after school when she was just fifteen, scooping ice cream to pay for the photographer and the clothes she needed, all the while hiding her passion from her parents. "They would have killed me if they knew I was doing any of this," explains Kiley.

Unfortunately, she had limited success in Atlanta. Countless auditions won her a few jobs handing out perfume in department stores, modeling clothes at a few events and even a couple of photo shoots for a local magazine. But it wasn't enough to satisfy Kiley. She still longed for the big time, success on the streets of New York. "I would lie in bed at night crying because I wanted to go to New York and be a big model," says Kiley. "But my parents wouldn't even talk to me about it."

So when Kiley spotted a newspaper ad for a local beauty contest awarding a New York modeling contract, she saw it as her big chance. "It said no experience necessary," remembers Kiley. "At first I thought it was a fake, but it said it would pay all expenses to New York for the finals and all that was needed to do was to show up, so I thought I'd check it out." She told Kent about the audition but swore him to secrecy.

Kiley took Kent to the contest, and as soon as she arrived and saw the glitzy production in full swing, she was sure she was on her way to fame and fortune. "They had the audition at a real exclusive hotel and everybody seemed nice," says Kiley. "All the girls there looked really pretty and famous and all that."

Kiley waited nervously for the contest to begin while Kent told her jokes to calm her down. Then it started. For three and a half hours Kiley walked, talked and smiled her heart out until the moment of truth arrived— the selection of the winners. As Kiley heard her name called out as one of the five girls picked, she cried and threw her arms around Kent. With ninety nine other girls from around the country, she would be flown to

New York City for the final competition. She was on top of the world. "All I cared about was that I was going to New York," remembers Kiley. "I didn't think about anything else. I just thought once I got there I would figure out the rest. I really was excited, and I thought I would win in New York, and the rest would be perfect."

But there was one problem—Kiley knew her parents would never allow her to go. So she forged their signatures on a release form and decided she'd go without telling them. She figured she'd only be gone a few days and when she got back with her big modeling contract, she could tell them how wrong they were about not letting her model. "They would have been furious and probably locked me in the closet if I told them before I left," says Kiley. "So I lied and ran away to do it. It all seemed perfectly simple to me then. I was pretty naïve." Only her friend Kent knew the truth, and though he was worried about her, he took her to the airport and saw her off, trusting that she would stay safe and come home as soon as the contest was over. "I wanted to go with her," says Kent. "I couldn't because of school, but I wanted her dreams to come true for her."

New York was everything Kiley thought it would be. The company put the girls up in an exclusive suite at a fancy hotel and gave them everything they wanted. For three days it was fun in the Big Apple—Broadway, Times Square, the Statue of Liberty; she saw it all.

Kiley's dream was coming true. Now all she had to do was beat out the other ninety-nine girls for the modeling contract.

But when the big day arrived, her dream was crushed before it even really got started. After only a one-minute walk out on a stage while cameras clicked and flashed, she was thanked and told to wait in back. An hour later she stood onstage while her name was called for dismissal along with eighty-nine other girls. She didn't even make the preliminary cut. "I was totally crushed," recalls Kiley. "I didn't even know what happened. I thought I must have done something wrong."

The next day she checked out of the hotel and waited for the bus to the airport, but while she sat in the lobby staring out the window at New York, she decided she couldn't go home. "My dreams were crushed, and I thought if I left now I would never make it, and my parents would crucify me for what I did. I thought this was my only chance." So Kiley checked into the cheapest motel she could find. But with less than $100 in her pocket, she knew she couldn't last there for more than a few days. She lied about her age and found a job as a waitress at a local coffee shop a day later. Then she called her friend Kent and her parents from a pay phone. "I told them all I was going to be famous and I didn't need them," explains Kiley. "I was angry, and I was going to prove I was special." Sadly, Kiley's parents' anger and harsh words destroyed any chance of luring her home. "My parents didn't even care about whether I was in some sleazy motel by myself—they just were angry that I lied and that I was modeling. Kent was the only one who cared, and I felt bad about him, but I figured he would understand."

Immediately she began going through all the local papers looking for modeling jobs and went to all the local agencies. But none of the real agencies were interested in Kiley and the less legitimate ones in the papers just wanted nude models or strippers. After a month of failure, she finally gave in to one of those ads. "I was really desperate," reveals Kiley, "and a guy at one of those agencies acted like he knew people in the real modeling business. He said if I did work for him he'd get me the work I wanted." For $100 Kiley agreed to model nude for some pictures for a phone sex ad. Less than a month later she was taking her clothes off for cash three days a week at a local strip club. She quit her job at the coffee shop and became a full-time nude model. "I needed the money," says Kiley. "And I figured nobody would ever know."

Meanwhile, back home her parents were trying to find her—just not very hard. Kent had given them all the information on the competition, and they contacted the authorities in New York City. Sadly, her strict and unforgiving father couldn't see past the fact that she lied and was modeling. So after a few calls and several inquiries, her parents did the incomprehensible and simply stopped looking. "I really think they never wanted to find me," says Kiley. "I never felt like they cared at all."

But her friend Kent was truly heartbroken. He was doing everything he could to track her down, from putting ads on the Internet to calling hotels, apartments and modeling agencies all over New York. But what he didn't realize was that she was now going by the name Sahara, and he was looking in the wrong places. "I knew she must have been in a lot of trouble," reveals Kent. "And her parents had deserted her essentially. I really loved her and I wanted to help her."

As Kiley's desire to become a model grew dimmer, her addiction to the New York street life grew. She began dating the men she danced for and got wrapped up in a life filled with cocaine and sex. Within less than six months she found out she was pregnant. "I just don't know how so much went so wrong so fast," explains Kiley. "But when I found out I was pregnant I knew I was at the bottom, especially when all the people I was associating with started telling me to just get rid of the baby, as if it was nothing." Kiley decided to keep the child, but as soon as she started to show, she lost her jobs, and the men with money and drugs vanished.

Back home, word of her whereabouts came to her parents and Kent in a most startling and shocking way: a censored version of one of her ads appeared in a local paper. "My dad was reading the sports section of the paper when he saw me in this tight little see-through outfit on this phone sex ad," reveals Kiley. "He immediately disowned me." Her father instructed his wife that from then on Kiley was never to be spoken of again in their house.

But when Kent heard about the ad from her parents, he was even more determined to find his friend. "There was no doubt in my mind, she'd wind up dead if I didn't help her," says Kent. The week after Kent graduated from high school, he set out for New York with $2,000 and the name of the company that had produced Kiley's ad. He decided he wouldn't go home until he found the girl he had loved since he was three years old. "She was so important to me, I didn't care what she had done," declares Kent. "I just wanted her to be safe, and if she needed me to rescue her then I would." The resourceful teen was turned away from the phone sex company the first time he tried to obtain any information on Kiley, but when he threatened to turn them in for using an underage girl for the explicit ads, they agreed to give him her contact information.

But the address was worthless because Kiley had already been kicked out of the cheap motel where she had been staying, and now she was aimlessly wandering the streets. "By that time I was completely broke," reveals Kiley. "I was living on the street, and let me tell you

being a pregnant drug addict on the street is no fun—
it's a living hell. I was so screwed up; I didn't know what
to do. The one place I knew I couldn't go was home to
my parents."

She walked the city streets looking for soup kitchens
and begging drug dealers for a place to sleep and a quick
fix. As she wandered down Broadway she suddenly heard
her name being called out by an all-too-familiar voice.
"I turned around and there was Kent, wearing the polo
shirt I gave him for Christmas one year," says Kiley. "It
was too small for him, but he sure looked good. I just
ran into his arms and hugged him." Kent had miraculously spotted Kiley after he checked out her former
apartment and immediately recognized her walking on
the street despite her changed appearance. "She was all
dirty and pregnant," says Kent. "But I didn't care. I loved
her, and I was ready to ask her to be my wife."

In the middle of Times Square Kent asked Kiley, bat-
tered and beaten by the streets and three months' pregnant, to marry him. She broke into tears. "Of course I
said yes," says Kiley. "I know I was pretty desperate at
the moment, but that wasn't it. I guess I just realized
that I had always loved him, but I didn't know how much
until that point. I knew we'd be happy together and that
he loved me more than anything."

Kent brought Kiley back to Atlanta, where they wed,
and six months later she gave birth to a beautiful baby

boy. They both enrolled in college the next year. Ten years later Kent is a successful engineer with his own business, and Kiley is a career counselor at a local high school. They have two children and are living happily ever after. "If it wasn't for Kent's love—I don't even want to think about what might have been," says Kiley. "I try every day to pass that love and understanding along to other young people in my job." Jokes Kiley, "I really have a 'model' life now and I love Kent and my children more than anything."

Puppy Love

~

Charlie felt as old as the hills by the time he hit sixty. His wife had died a few years earlier, his children were all off and married with families of their own and he really didn't want to be bothered with meeting anyone new.

But there was only one problem with Charlie's plan of keeping to himself: he was lonely. "I really couldn't stand being in that house all by myself," remembers Charlie. "So I decided a dog would be a perfect companion." He wasn't picky about the type of dog and he figured something that might grow into a good watchdog would be nice to protect his property.

So Charlie went down to the local pound. And after

looking through what seemed like a million dogs he spotted his pooch. "He was a tough little rottweiler scrapper trying to eat through the cage, and he was all wrecked up," reveals Charlie. "His eye was all smashed in and he wasn't pretty, but he had so much spunk. I knew that was my dog." Charlie's dog had been beaten up by street kids after being abandoned by his owner. He would eventually recover most of his faculties, and the injuries would all heal except for that one eye, which was permanently blinded.

Charlie took the dog home and began training him. "He quickly learned where to go and where not to go," says Charlie. "He was a real good dog. I knew I had made the right choice." Charlie named him Eyegor for his bad eye and because he looked hunched over when he walked sometimes, just like the assistant in the old horror movies. Charlie slowly nursed his new pal back to health, and Eyegor soon became Charlie's constant companion and best friend. "He was there all the time, following me wherever I went in the house. I certainly was never going to be lonely around him. He'd even follow me into the bathroom!"

The two grew so close, Eyegor couldn't stand it whenever Charlie left the house without him. Once when Charlie had a doctor's appointment, his faithful pup even broke through the back window to be with him! "I had to go to the doctor and I figured it wasn't the place for him," recalls Charlie. "I didn't get maybe ten feet out the door when I saw him through the window, jumping up and down like crazy. He wound up breaking through the glass to be with me. I guess he felt I saved his life or something."

Once when a friend came over to play cards and suggested he put Eyegor out, doting Charlie came up with a better idea. "I told the guy he could leave," explains Charlie. "Nobody was going to tell my dog to leave. As far as I was concerned, that house was his house as much as mine."

Charlie and his pet pooch spent the next nine years growing old together. They were never apart, sleeping together, eating together, watching TV together and even playing golf together. "We had each other and that's all we needed," says Charlie. "That dog made me feel like a little kid."

The day after Charlie's seventieth birthday was a frigid January morning. As he had done every day for nearly forty years, he started the day by putting a pot of coffee on the stove, popping a piece of toast in the toaster and letting Eyegor out the back door for his morning ritual. Then he went upstairs to turn the heat up in the house and take a shower. As Eyegor took care of business outside, Charlie cleaned up inside.

But Charlie was unaware that a dish towel had fallen onto the toaster in the kitchen and ignited. In seconds the wooden cabinets were on fire, and the kitchen quickly became an inferno. Within minutes, most of the house was on fire. With the doors to the bedroom and bathroom both shut and the heater turned up, Charlie was unaware that fire had engulfed the rest of the house. After getting out of the shower he walked out into his bedroom and thought he smelled smoke.

As he opened his bedroom door to walk downstairs and search out the source of the odor, a deadly wall of smoke overcame him. He lost his balance, blacked out and slipped on the stairs. As flames engulfed the house, Charlie's faithful companion, Eyegor, frantically barked and pounded his body against the back door of the house, trying to get in.

Neighbors didn't notice the fire until Eyegor's non-stop yelping and barking sent them running out of their houses to see what was wrong. They quickly called 911, realizing it was too dangerous for them to go into the house themselves. But crucial minutes would pass before the fire department arrived.

Eyegor continued to try and get in the house, while neighbors tried to calm him. "He was insane," reveals a neighbor who witnessed the dog's tirade. "He just wouldn't stop trying to get back in there. We tried to hold him back. But when a rottweiler has his mind made up you don't try and stop him."

The house continued to fill with smoke while Charlie

lay unconscious on his stairway. A window burst from the heat just as the fire department pulled up, and Eyegor suddenly made a furious running leap through the broken window into the house. "I have never seen a dog jump like that," explains another neighbor. "And into a burning building—it was the most incredible thing I've ever witnessed."

Eyegor somehow made it through the asphyxiating smoke and deadly flames to find Charlie within seconds. "I don't remember anything but suddenly he was biting my arm hard," says Charlie. "I mean it hurt bad. But it woke me up quick." Charlie grabbed his beloved Eyegor, covered his face with his bath towel and dashed toward the door. Just seconds after they tumbled out the back door, the roof collapsed and the structure crashed to the ground.

Paramedics and firemen grabbed both of them and checked for injuries. They took Charlie to the hospital, with Eyegor right beside him at Charlie's insistence. Firefighters on the scene later confirmed that the spot where Charlie fell was directly underneath a major beam in the roof that had collapsed and surely would have killed him.

Now Charlie has changed his will to provide for Eyegor when he's gone by donating a portion of the proceeds from the sale of his new home to a fund for Eyegor's care.

"Eyegor saved my life," says Charlie. "And I'll do whatever I can to make that dog as happy he can be until the day he dies. That's the least I can do for my best pal."

A Hog for Love!

❧

*J*oAnn never thought she'd be the owner of a one-hundred-fifty-pound potbellied pig. A homemaker and Republican committee fund-raiser in her hometown of Beaver Falls, Pennsylvania, the sixty-year-old had plenty on her plate to keep her busy when she wasn't taking care of her foundry worker husband, Jack.

But with her children finally raised and out of the house, she and her husband decided it was finally time to begin enjoying some quality time alone with each other, and so they began taking frequent weekend getaways to nearby Lake Erie. There her husband would fish and she would just take in the fresh air and relax.

They were looking forward to the best years of their lives.

But life wasn't perfect for JoAnn. When doctors diagnosed her cancer a few years back, she began radiation therapy. But to make matters worse, she started having heart problems. After her first heart attack in 1997, she was rushed into emergency surgery. "They said the surgery would fix everything," recalls JoAnn. "And I felt like I was better after I got out of the hospital, so I figured they were right."

A few months later, LuLu waddled into her life. The black-and-white bountiful beauty first appeared on her doorstep when her husband bought LuLu as a peculiar present for their daughter, Jackie. But JoAnn didn't think this was such a great gift for their forty-year-old banker daughter. "I didn't know what he was thinking," says JoAnn. "I mean, she wasn't the type to keep a pig."

And JoAnn was right. Almost immediately after naming her LuLu, Jackie started pawning the piggy off on her parents when she and her husband went on their frequent weekend trips. Finally Jackie stopped picking her up altogether, and LuLu began to win JoAnn's heart. "We grew very attached to each other," reveals JoAnn. "Whenever we tried to give her back she started crying. That's when I decided she was staying with us."

JoAnn's new friend was just like a child, sneaking in

the refrigerator when she wasn't looking, watching television and running errands with JoAnn. JoAnn really started attracting attention when she and LuLu would lay out together at the beach, working on their tans. And when they were at home LuLu's favorite place to be was in JoAnn's lap. "And remember this was a one-hundred-fifty-pound pig," jokes JoAnn. "That's no lightweight." JoAnn and her husband, Jack, loved LuLu's company so much that they even began taking LuLu with them on weekend getaways along with their American Eskimo dog, Bear. So when they headed off to Lake Erie in the summer of 1998 for some fishing and fun, LuLu and Bear came along for the ride.

The day after they arrived, Jack got up early and headed out on the lake to catch dinner, allowing JoAnn to sleep in. But a few hours later when she rose to get out of bed she suddenly collapsed. "I passed out three times while trying to get up out of bed," says JoAnn. "Each time I came to, I'd try to get up again. But the third time I fell to the floor, and I felt my left arm go numb. That's when I knew it was a heart attack." As JoAnn lay helpless on the floor, Bear, the rescue dog, did nothing, but LuLu came frantically running to her aid. Like the faithful companion that she was, LuLu stood by her fallen master's side and used her huge head to try and nudge JoAnn into getting up. But when JoAnn didn't move, LuLu began nervously pacing back and forth.

181

"She knew immediately that something was very wrong," says JoAnn, "and she was hysterical about it."

JoAnn couldn't move, and she knew with her husband unreachable, her only chance would be to cry for help and hope someone in the trailer park would hear her. She let out the loudest scream she could muster in her feeble condition. Then she waited. But, incredibly, none of the nearly one thousand people in the park came to her rescue. "After a few minutes I knew nobody was coming," says JoAnn. "That's when I realized I was going to die!" Without any way to get help, JoAnn lost all hope. "My whole life flashed before my eyes, from kindergarten on. And I started asking out loud for God to forgive me. At that point I had given up on life."

Except LuLu wasn't ready to give up on her beloved friend. She paced faster and faster back and forth in the trailer, frantically butting JoAnn over and over again with her big head. "The longer I lay there on that floor, the crazier she got," remembers JoAnn. "I knew she was out of her mind because she sensed I was dying." But even as JoAnn faced her final moments she had LuLu's best interest at heart, ordering her to leave the room so she wouldn't witness the horrible sight of her owner's passing. "I didn't want her to have to watch me die," says JoAnn. "So I looked at her and told her I loved her, then I asked her go lie down in the other room and go 'nite-nite.' "

As soon as JoAnn told her to leave the room, LuLu began crying like a baby. "Tears started streaming down her cheeks," recalls JoAnn. "I felt so bad because I knew she loved me so much. I was asking out loud for God to take care of my husband and LuLu."

JoAnn knew LuLu was desperate to help, but she could never have imagined what the loving and loyal pig did next! To JoAnn's complete astonishment, suddenly LuLu made a mad break for the front door of the trailer, and with all her might the portly pig busted through the tiny doggie door, seriously wounding herself on the way. "I was totally blown away," remembers JoAnn. "She was going crazy because she didn't want me to die, and I knew how much she must have been hurting." Despite JoAnn's own pain, she was still more concerned about LuLu. Bloodied, LuLu ran half a block away into the oncoming traffic of a busy street, risking her own life to gain the attention of motorists whizzing by in their cars. The potbellied savior was dwarfed by the cars. Dodging the speeding vehicles, LuLu tried everything she could to get someone to stop and follow her to her fallen master. But no matter how hard she tried nobody would stop.

LuLu charged back and forth along the busy street, narrowly avoiding being hit, and then back into the trailer park in a futile attempt to get somebody to follow her. Then she ran back to the trailer to check up on her owner, who was fading fast. "She was a real mess with blood when she came back," recalls JoAnn, "and I felt so bad for her. But I knew it was the end. What was a pig going to do?"

The loving pig refused to give up on her lady. She returned to the busy thoroughfare, again risking her life for JoAnn. This time, she stood firm right in the middle of the road determined to get somebody's attention. The massive stream of cars swerved to avoid her, but still not a soul would stop. Then, in a final act of desperation, she lay down on the road ready to die in her last attempt to stop a motorist. Cars screeched to a halt to avoid hitting the sprawled-out pig. Then finally someone came to help poor LuLu.

LuLu immediately sprang to her feet and led the driver back to JoAnn's trailer where, amazingly, she was still alive and conscious. Suddenly JoAnn heard the welcome sound of a human voice. " 'Your pig is in distress,' the man called out from the door," remembers JoAnn. "That's when I screamed, 'Help me, I'm having a heart attack.' " The passerby quickly ran to the campground office and dialed 911. An ambulance arrived within minutes to rush JoAnn to the nearest hospital.

While paramedics scrambled to save JoAnn, another tended to the pig's wounds, but LuLu still refused to leave JoAnn's side. "She kept diving for the ambulance," recalls JoAnn. "She actually was crying at the ambulance door as they shut it. She even tried climbing up on the back bumper. She was determined to save me, and she wanted to see for herself I was safe. That's how much she loved me." The ambulance reached the hospital with not a moment to spare. "The doctor told me if it had been another two minutes later, I would have been dead," reveals JoAnn. "LuLu saved my life."

After three weeks in intensive care and successful open-heart surgery, JoAnn returned home to the loving grunts of her pig. As soon as JoAnn entered the house, the passionate pig broke through the storm door and came running into the house. "She jumped up on me, and we both cried," recalls JoAnn. "I wouldn't be here if it wasn't for LuLu."

Now the pig and her proprietress are best friends and are never parting. "I know LuLu saved my life," declares JoAnn. "And I'll never stop loving her for it. I told my husband we're not giving LuLu back to our daughter, not ever. She's staying right here with me. And he says that's just fine with him."

Purrfect Love

*J*osie was never a big star. Since she was seventeen, she had made a comfortable living as a local ballerina in San Francisco and even had her own studio where she taught many an aspiring star the meaning of grace and beauty. "I loved ballet more than anything else in the world," says Josie. "That's why I never married. It was my life."

Nor did Josie have any children, or even a boyfriend for the most part. She was always too busy trying to make ends meet and turning her passion into some kind of a dependable career. From the time she was three, when she had her first ballet lesson, dancing was all Josie ever cared about. While other little girls wanted dolls,

Josie wanted toe shoes and pink leotards. She stuck with ballet, performing through college, and when she graduated with a fine arts degree, she knew dancing was all she ever wanted to do.

She began teaching at community college and dancing in local productions. She was happy and very fulfilled and hoped to eventually break onto the national scene and make a name for herself in the world of contemporary dance.

As the years passed Josie began to realize she would never hit the big time as a performer. But that was still all right because she loved teaching and working with local theaters. When she wasn't dancing, she was traveling all over the country to watch acclaimed productions and visit renowned dance theater groups, where she'd meet other dancers and learn how to choreograph and direct.

With no brothers, sisters or true friends to speak of, her parents were her only real anchor to anything in the world outside of dance. "They always loved and supported my decision to be a dancer rather than take the traditional route in life," says Josie. "I loved them so much for that. They were really all I had besides my dancing."

When Josie was thirty-eight, she started her own studio while still performing and choreographing for community theaters all over Northern California. For the next decade, she worked harder than she had ever worked in her life. To keep herself in exquisite physical shape, she woke every day at 5 A.M., ran two miles, stretched for an hour, then practiced her own routines for another hour. Then she ate breakfast, showered and got to her studio by 9 A.M. for her first class and taught straight through to 10 P.M. Three days a week she also either performed, choreographed or directed local productions. "Most women I knew thought there was something wrong with me," reveals Josie, "because I didn't want what they had: the two kids and the husband and the dog and all that. That's one reason why I didn't have any friends. No one could understand that I loved dancing as much as other women loved being moms or wives."

By the time she was forty-nine, most of those woman were watching their children go off to college while they were getting ready to settle down with their husbands into early retirement. But Josie was getting ready to go on tour as a choreographer for a national ballet company. "I always wanted to tour," says Josie. "I never got a chance as a performer, but it didn't matter. The chance to choreograph was just as great." But as she prepared to make her dreams come true, a series of events turned Josie's life into a real-life tragedy. First Josie's mother died after a massive heart attack just two days before the first performance. Josie was devastated.

Touring would have to wait while Josie mourned and tried to overcome the tremendous pain of losing the mother she loved with all her heart and the only woman she could ever talk to. "She was really my only girl-friend," says Josie. "We used to share everything together, and she was always there for me." Josie immediately went home to be with her father and attend to the funeral and the burial.

Then, incredibly, just two days later her father died in his sleep of a massive embolism. Josie was in complete shock! "My parents were the only thing I loved more than my ballet," says Josie. "It was a nightmare, and I couldn't wake up. My whole world was turned upside down, and I didn't know what to do."

Now Josie was alone in the world. Devastated by her parents' deaths and with her only support system gone, she fell into deep despair and grief. The only thing she had left to take her mind off her pain was her dancing. So she arranged to rejoin the tour as an assistant choreographer as soon as possible.

But things would get worse still for Josie when two months later she was diagnosed as being in the beginning stages of multiple sclerosis. She was given two years at the most before the crippling and immobilizing effects of the neuromuscular disease would begin to take their toll. "It was a death sentence for me," remembers Josie. "I had no family, no friends, no nothing. All I had was my body and my mind and the beauty I could make with them, and now that was threatened too."

She tried every doctor, every remedy, and every precaution but soon the effects were felt. By the time she was fifty-three, she was confined to a wheelchair and forced to give up dancing. Within another year she was losing upper body control. Unable to even teach any longer she gave up the studio as well. She was alone and terrified of the future, and soon her thoughts grew desperate. "I was getting worse and worse every day, and there was nobody to take care of me. I felt so depressed that I started thinking about killing myself. Suddenly it seemed like the only way out of my pain."

One day while planning her demise, her parents' old neighbors appeared at her door carrying a small, furry white kitten. It was the offspring of her mother's cat, which they had taken in when she died. The neighbors thought the sweet little critter would be a perfect companion for lonely Josie. But she was in such deep despair, she didn't even want to look at the kitten, let alone adopt her. "I was getting ready to throw in the towel," remembers Josie, "and they show up with this kitten. It was absurd. Besides, how was I supposed to take care of a cat when I couldn't even take care of myself?"

When the neighbors insisted, she agreed to take her, naming her Twinkles because of her dainty disposition. But Josie was still very serious about her death wish. She decided on a date, a method and a place for her suicide. She even wrote out the note she would leave by her body. She would use sleeping pills, and she wanted to be found in her living room surrounded by the pictures of her dancing over the years.

Meanwhile, Twinkles was becoming an undeniable joy to Josie. Every day she woke Josie up by nibbling on her ear. And at night she'd jump on her bed and serenade Josie to sleep with the gentle sound of her purr. "I was definitely getting attached to her," reveals Josie. "And that bothered me because I kept thinking about what would happen to her after I was gone. She was filling a void in my life, and it felt good. I was falling in love with her. But I still felt totally hopeless and wanted to kill myself."

Twinkles and Josie became inseparable. And Josie did everything she could for the cat. Twinkles gave Josie a reason to get up in the morning. When Josie discovered how much Twinkles loved playing with string, she tied a cord to her wheelchair so she could chase Josie around the house all day and play. As the date of Josie's planned suicide drew closer, she grew even more worried over what would happen to her Twinkles when she was gone. "It seemed like every time I would think about ending my life or making a plan the cat would find me and nuzzle up next to me," explains Josie. "It was remarkable. It was as if she could read my mind. I didn't want anything to happen to her. I wanted somebody nice to take her." Josie arranged for someone from one of her old theater groups to come over the day before she killed herself to take the cat, claiming she had to go into the hospital for a few days. "I thought if somebody took her before it happened, they'd probably keep her."

But as the fateful day drew closer, so did Twinkles to Josie. One morning when Josie broke down crying, Twinkles popped up on her lap and raised her paw to Josie's eyes as if to wipe away the tears. "It was an eerie thing—she was feeling my pain," swears Josie. "She was waking something in my heart that I thought had died with my dancing."

As the day of her planned suicide approached, she readied her will, tied up her loose ends and prepared for the end. Then suddenly Josie heard a loud crash coming from the bathroom. At first she feared a burglar had broken in. But when she wheeled herself to see, she found Twinkles up on the sink with the medicine cabinet pried open. She had knocked over a glass soap dish when she jumped up on the sink. But it was what the feline did next that changed Josie's life forever.

"While I'm staring at her wondering what's up, she actually reached up and knocked down the bottle of pills I was planning on using to kill myself," reveals Josie. "All I know is everything changed in my heart right then and I threw out the pills."

Josie was spiritually transformed by Twinkles's devotion. Feeling much more hopeful, Josie changed her life the very next day. Though still in a wheelchair, she made plans to teach a dance class at a local community center with the aid of an assistant. She started volunteering her time at a hospice to help people with AIDS. She began writing poetry and she wrote a textbook on dance for the community college.

Though her MS continued to deteriorate her abilities, the next year she received a standing ovation for choreographing a student production at the local community center theater. And when Josie wheeled herself onto the stage to accept the applause, she wasn't alone. She had one very loved white cat in her arms.

Chris Benguhe has extensive experience as a professional writer and has served as the entertainment and lifestyle writer for such publications as *People* magazine. He has also worked as the Editor-in-Chief of several magazines, including his own arts and entertainment magazine in Scottsdale, Arizona. He has also ghostwritten several books. Chris currently lives in Boca Raton, Florida, where he works as a writer and editor.